CHASI...

For Gene

With warmest
wishes &
gratitude.

Michael Cassidy

Mar '87

By the same author:

WHERE ARE YOU TAKING THE WORLD ANYWAY?
BURSTING THE WINESKINS

CHASING THE WIND

Man's Search for Life's Answers

Michael Cassidy

HODDER AND STOUGHTON
LONDON SYDNEY AUCKLAND TORONTO

British Library Cataloguing in Publication Data

Cassidy, Michael
  Chasing the wind; man's search for life's
  answers. – –(Hodder Christian paperbacks)
  1. Christian life
  I. Title
  248.4   BV4501.2

ISBN 0 340 37425 X

*Copyright © 1985 by Michael Cassidy. First printed 1985. Second impression 1985.
All rights reserved. No part of this publication may be reproduced or transmitted in any
form or by any means, electronic or mechanical, including photocopy, recording, or any
information storage and retrieval system, without permission in writing from the
publisher. Printed in Great Britain for Hodder and Stoughton Limited, Mill Road,
Dunton Green, Sevenoaks, Kent by Hunt Barnard Printing Ltd., Aylesbury, Bucks.*

Hodder and Stoughton Editorial Office. 47 Bedford Square, London WC1B 3DP.

But as I looked at everything I had tried, it was all so useless, a chasing of the wind, and there was nothing really worthwhile anywhere.

> Solomon – Eccles. 2:11 LB

Just as you can hear the wind but can't tell where it comes from or where it will go next, so it is with the Spirit. We do not know on whom he will next bestow this life from heaven.

> Jesus – John 3:7–8 LB

Carol, who helps make my

writing possible, joins me

in dedicating this volume

to our children – Catherine
Deborah
and Martin

and godchildren –

Andrew Bester
Juliet Baber
Sharon Ducker
Paula Evans
Graeme Hodgson
James Macaulay
Susan Millard
Lisa Peace
Liesel Welland
Nicholas Welsh
(Mine)

Richard Evans
David Hewson
Jonathan Le Feuvre
Olivia Mitchell
Catherine Pickering
(Hers)

not forgetting Michael Fyvie
who has already Gone Ahead.

Author's Preface

I have written this book for those who feel they are seeking for a living faith, but who are not sure if Christianity is really true or if it can solve their problems or meet their needs for purpose, peace and joy. My hope is that these pages will assist them along the way and lead them into life's most glorious discovery, that of finding Christ as Saviour, Lord and friend.

I hope the book will also encourage and strengthen Christians and help them share with others 'the reason for the Hope that is in them'.

To thank all those on whose thoughts and insights I have drawn for this volume would be both difficult and tedious, but I would pay special tribute to the late Stephen Neill of Wycliffe Hall, Oxford, who over eighteen years was a deeply valued friend, counsellor and mentor to me. He influenced and encouraged me beyond what words can readily express. In this volume I honour his memory.

Deep gratitude must also go to Nellis du Preez and Wessel Dirksen who read and reread the manuscript countless times and gave huge help in the shaping and editing of the book. Other assistance came from Anthea Tasker and Malcolm Graham. Professor George Quicke, a biochemist, and Dr Rob Caldwell, my physician, made excellent suggestions about the sections touching on science and faith. Invaluable counsel, based on extensive publishing experience, also came to me from Carolyn Armitage, Rob Warner and Edward England, whose creative insights were often decisive in helping me refine the book into its final form. Bertha Graham of the Africa Enterprise computer department deserves particular appreciation as she has put in countless untiring hours of labour on our word processor to get the final copy of the typescript in shape. Jenny Johnn, my secretary, has also helped greatly at many points along the way. To all these valued colleagues and friends I owe a deep debt of gratitude.

Finally I must reserve my ultimate thanks for my dear wife Carol who endlessly takes up the slack at home, thereby releasing me to give time for writing. Her sacrifices on this front are real and many and I salute her for her loving and dedicated spirit. I know she cares as much as I that many should come to know Christ as Lord and Saviour through what is written in these pages.

Michael Cassidy
Pietermaritzburg, South Africa, November 1984

Contents

Chapter One

WHAT'S IT ALL ABOUT?

I haven't a clue who Peter Sellers is.
Peter Sellers

I was at Kennedy Airport just about to board a plane en route back to South Africa. I had just clambered, bags and all, on to an airport limousine along with about ten others, to be driven to the departure terminal. That was when I met him. One of the most unforgettable characters I ever encountered. Life to him was just a ball. He was living it with a capital L.

As most of my fellow-travellers vanished behind the *New York Times*, a voice rang out, 'Mornin' everyone.' It was the driver. I peered round the stock-market page of the preoccupied passenger beside me and saw a jovial black with a huge smile climbing into the driver's seat.

He surveyed the dismal offering of passengers which the early morning had presented to him. A few grunts of response was his only reward. 'Morning,' I said, somewhat bashfully.

'Well, at least ah'm happy,' he chortled, thereby pronouncing his considered verdict on the state of the rest of us!

Feeling I ought to try and rise to the occasion on behalf of the rest of humanity I ventured a friendly comment.

'Got a long day ahead?' I asked.

'Well, man,' he drawled with that extra special and

inimitable accent of a Brooklyn black, 'I've have been on
from 1 a.m. and I got till 9 a.m. Dat's ma shift, you see. But
it may be longer; dey may call me for extra. You know, dey
pull dem tricks sometimes. But dat's okay. You see, it's de
service dat counts. You gotta give dat service good, man,
real good.'

The sentence tailed off in some more deep chuckles
rumbling up from his middle abdomen and then
tumbling out like a tonic on the frosty world around him.

'Goodness,' I thought to myself, 'this chap's got it. He's
a demonstrator. He's a preacher who practises what he
preaches. He is a taximan who is concerned to render true
service in the one way he knows how – driving his
limousine the best and happiest way he can.'

'Yeah, man,' he went on, as if reflecting on the triumph
of his spirit over the nature of his job. 'I guess I's de only
guy around here wot can make dis job a heck of a lot of
fun!' More roars of semi-philosophical laughter.

I continued thinking, 'It's unbelievable. He's been up
since 1 a.m. He should be ready to spit in everybody's eye,
and here he is right on form, so full of fun and blessing the
world.'

We then began arriving at different air terminals where
various passengers would disembark.

'Anyone for Sunlight over Jordan?' he called out. 'Dat's
Eastern Airlines!'

A couple of disgruntled commuters spilled out. We
drove on.

'What about Alcoholics Anonymous? Dat's AA.
American Airlines. Okay, no one for AA.'

'Now,' said the tonic, warming to his game, 'how 'bout
"Fussy on de Ground"?'

I looked suitably perplexed and rose to his bait like any
good trout.

'Dat's United, friendly in de sky – fussy on de ground!'
He beamed seraphically as we all clicked in recollection of
the slogan, 'Fly the friendly skies of United'.

'Oh, brother,' I mused to myself, 'keep preaching.

That's us religious people. Friendly in the skies of church, fussy on the ground during the week!'

'Now Needle Nose,' he announced with finality. 'Dat's British Airways. You know dey got dat plane with de long nose. Oh, man! To see dat baby land! Bootiful!'

I disembarked at Needle Nose, wistfully wishing I was flying the Concorde! As my new friend got my bags out, I said to him round at the back of the limousine, 'You've got an inner secret. You must be a Christian.'

Now his face just exploded in wrinkles of delight.

'Yessir,' he beamed, his eyes sparkling and popping even wider, 'He's made me da greatest lover in da world! He did something mighty for ma life thirty-two years ago and He also gave me a commandment, yessir, a commandment, "lerv everybody as ah have lerved yew". Dat's right. Everybody. Ma name's Mitty, sir. Just call me Mitty.'

'Oh, Mitty,' I said, 'you've made my day.'

And he had.

ENVY

Strange, isn't it? Every now and then one meets people who have somehow just got it. And we envy them. Not that they all have irrepressible personalities like Mitty. But they've got something. An inner secret. A sort of 'got the act together and on top of life' impression. Somehow they seem at peace with themselves and the world. They're at home in the universe. And we want what they've got. Because we too want to live life to the full.

But somehow that sense of meaning eludes us. We wonder what it's all about, but no answers seem to come. We can't get our relationships to work properly. We fumble along without purpose. And most perplexing of all, we can't quite figure out who we ourselves actually are.

Not long before his death Peter Sellers, one of the most

talented and successful comic actors in the history of film, remarked to a friend: 'I haven't a clue who Peter Sellers is.' This fellow who could take off any character and keep an audience rolling in the aisles added: 'I have no personality of my own. I reached my present position by working hard and not following Socrates' advice "Know thyself". I couldn't follow it if I wanted to. To me, I am a complete stranger.'

According to his fourth wife, actress Lynne Frederick, his mind was 'in a constant state of turmoil about what his purpose was on this planet and whether it was all worth while.'

In fact Sellers's preoccupation with identity and meaning manifested itself in a determination to play the part of Chance in the film *Being There* which won him an academy award nomination in the year he died. Chance was a reclusive gardener whose only knowledge of the world came from television. Sellers thought this eerily mirrored his own feeling that he was out of touch with the real world and with himself.

YOU AND YOUR MIRROR

Ever felt that way? Perhaps you have caught yourself, as many others have, early in the morning, looking in the mirror at that dishevelled bundle of sleepiness and muzz which is you! You're just about to shave or wash or put on some make-up or brush your hair, or whatever, and you suddenly pause as you see your reflection in the mirror. The bleary face stares at you and you stare back.

'Who are you?', you ask.

'Wouldn't you like to know?' echoes back the image.

Something very strange is happening. You are becoming aware of both the self staring into the mirror and the self reflected in the mirror.

'That's ever so odd,' you reflect, as you blink the muzziness out of those blood-shot eyes that look as if you'd just slept overnight in the Gobi desert, 'but I am aware almost of a second me, a self outside space and time, which is seeing both me and my reflection.'

Then you snap yourself back to reality. Darn it! You feel like the morning after the night before, yet you haven't been anywhere! Anyway, time to get on with the business of your morning ablutions!

But when you stop to think about it, that sort of experience is actually very mysterious. It is also very important because it makes us realise that somehow we humans are the great amphibians between nature and that which is above or beyond nature. It's all very strange. And it gets stranger when we start asking questions such as 'Who really am I? What sort of creature is this which can reflect about itself, enjoy music, appreciate the *Mona Lisa*, marvel at the sunset, get outraged at Col. Gaddafi, and get scared to death going down a narrow road with a reckless driver?'

All this makes us ask even more – 'What's it all about?' Perhaps even beyond that, it is the question of meaning which drives us ever more vigorously in the pursuit of happiness, joy and fulfilment in life. And so we become ready to give anything a go. Wishing all the time that we could end up just a bit like Mitty, the irrepressible and joyous taxi-driver!

Chapter Two

CHASING THE WIND

> I looked at everything I had tried. It was all so useless – a
> chasing of the wind, and there was nothing really worth
> while anywhere.
>
> Solomon – Eccles. 2:11

I remember years ago reading an amazing story by Honoré
de Balzac, the great nineteenth-century French novelist. It
was called *The Wild Ass's Skin*. It was all about an eager,
seeking young man to whom a French shopkeeper wanted
to sell an ass's skin with magical properties. It worked like
this. If the young man purchased the skin he could make
any wish while holding the ass's skin and it would come
true – but with each wish the skin would shrink just a little
bit. When the skin finally shrank to nothing the young
man would die. He could either have a long, dull
pedestrian life, or a short one lived to the full, whatever
that would mean in his understanding and according to
his choices.

The young man weighs up the alternatives. Finally like
a flower bursting into blossom, he says '*Je veux vivre avec
excès*' which literally means 'I want to live life to excess,'
or 'I want to live life to the very full, abundantly.'

And so the die is cast and an incredible saga of magically
granted self-indulgent living follows. This finally shrinks
both the skin and his own life to a tragic zero. His wishes
are all granted, but happiness eludes him. He has lived to

excess, but it came to naught. It ended in a deathly cul-de-sac.

Yet which of us could not identify with the young man's wish 'I want to live life to excess – abundantly.' The wish was sound enough, natural enough, instinctive enough. Nothing wrong with that. But gratifying self and its desires just doesn't bring fulfilment. Only a dead-end.

SOLOMON

Of course to get whatever one wants is the sort of thing which to most people stays in the realm of fairies and magic wands. But every now and then people do appear who are in a position to get whatever they want. One of these is spoken about in the Bible itself. The fellow's name was Solomon and he tells us his story in a book of the Bible called Ecclesiastes. As King of Israel, one of the richest men who ever lived, and a man of keen desire to know what life was all about, he is in a pretty good position to say something meaningful to us.

First of all he tells us 'I said to myself, "Come now, be merry; enjoy yourself to the full"' (2:1a). He wanted to test the life of pleasure by just enjoying himself as much as he possibly could. To test a plane you fly it. To test a recipe, you prepare the food and eat it. To test a swing, you swing on it. To test pleasure, you taste it and try it and abandon yourself to it.

Multitudes of frenzied moderns try this way. Yet all they find, to come back to Balzac, is that 'diving to the bottom of pleasure, we bring up more gravel than pearls.' Said Solomon at the end of his pleasure cruise 'I found that this, too, was futile' (2:1b).

Then he tried comedy – 'laughter', as he called it. Now who doesn't love a good giggle? In fact, a hilarious evening over a good comedy is as good a tonic as our tired old world can throw up. Martin Luther thought so highly of laughter that he vowed 'If you're not allowed to laugh in Heaven, I don't want to go there.'

But laughter and humour, as we saw with poor Peter Sellers, is hopeless on its own as an escape from the vale of tears which is planet earth. Commented Solomon – 'It is silly to be laughing all the time; what good does it do?' (2:2 LB).

Solomon presses on further. 'After a lot of thinking I decided to try the road of drink' (2:3). He was not the first, nor was he the last. For some this is pure escapism. Asked why he hit the bottle as he did, one British drunk replied: 'It's the fastest way out of Manchester!'

For others it is not the way of escapism so much as it is the way of personality release. I know one shy fellow who can hardly get two words together when you meet him stone-cold sober. But after a good few drinks he becomes the magnetic, pulsating, devil-may-care life and soul of the party.

However, the kicks have the kickback and the unreal answer is followed by constant very rude awakenings to life's very real problems. My friend will vouch for that.

It's the same with drugs – described by one doctor as 'death on the instalment plan'.

Aldous Huxley in his *Brave New World* described a technocratic society in which a drug called Soma is regularly taken by supermen to counteract their fears and feelings of meaninglessness. And certainly today there are many who hope by taking drugs to experience the reality of something which will give life some meaning.

But the price of any temporary increase of perception is too high. Beginning in the senses and ending with the senses, drugs cannot transcend physical reality. They just shatter it.

Such are the ways of escape.

PUBLIC OR PROFESSIONAL SERVICE

Solomon had yet another ploy up his sleeve. 'Then I tried to find fulfilment by inaugurating a great public works programme: homes, vineyards, gardens, parks and orchards for myself and reservoirs to hold the water to irrigate my plantations' (2:4–6).

Now, we must hand it to this fellow – he was a person of pretty astonishing resourcefulness. He didn't just sit back as far as his quest went. With incredible energy he got stuck into a mass of ambitious public schemes. Imagine how he must have been admired, envied, marvelled at.

Yet inside, Solomon by his own testimony remained unhappy and dissatisfied.

Many big-time moderns in the political and professional worlds try this route too.

Once I spent an hour with a senior political figure in what was then Rhodesia (now Zimbabwe). We talked about Central African politics for a while and then he asked me about my work. I told him about the challenges and joys of sharing Christ with people.

A pensive, distant and almost wistful expression suddenly gripped his face.

'I envy you,' he responded in a quiet tone. In spite of holding political power something was still missing in his life. Public prominence, and in his instance considerable economic achievement in his country, had still left his soul barren and bereft.

Many who serve in the professional sphere, rather than civic or political, know this feeling too. They work as lawyers, doctors, accountants, nurses, teachers or whatever and in many ways they seem to be leading fulfilled lives, but backstage in their souls they are saying 'So what?' It has all become a meaningless round. As the Southern States ditch-digger replied when asked why he was digging the ditch: 'I digga da ditch to getta da money to buya da food to getta da strength to digga da ditch!'

The fact is that every person, whether in the professions or out of them, whether powerful or powerless, high or low, educated or illiterate, is sooner or later driven to ask the big questions and to seek deliverance from the meaningless round.

RELAXED AND WEALTHY

Now he tries another ploy. 'Next I bought slaves, both men and women... I also bred great herds and flocks, more than any of the kings before me. I collected silver and gold as taxes from many kings and provinces' (2:7-8).

With servants galore he could sit back and relax. Beyond that he accumulated vast wealth. Lucky fellow. No worries about his fuel bills, or spiralling inflation. Sounds marvellous. But Solomon didn't find it so. He concluded,

> He who loves money shall never have enough... The more you have the more you spend, right up to the limits of your income, so what is the advantage of wealth - except perhaps to watch it as it runs through your fingers! The man who works hard sleeps well, whether he eats little or much, but the rich must worry and suffer insomnia (5:10-11).

He then adds that 'investments also turn sour'. In the end all one's wealth gets whittled down and one ends up 'gloomy, discouraged, frustrated and angry' (5:13-17).

A businessman I know told me his wealth gave him constant anxiety and worry until he found a spiritual framework for life. Then his wealth became a beautiful asset for life and service and generosity to others. But he had to find something 'bigger than boodle' to make any of it add up to anything.

Solomon found this too. This whole enterprise was 'like chasing the wind' (1:18), he commented.

Even so, he kept it up for a while. There were still many other things to try.

MUSIC

Solomon put it this way. 'In the cultural arts, I organised men's and women's choirs and orchestras' (2:8b).

Oh, but music is wonderful! Culture generally and

music specifically bring such delights to the human heart. I mean, just imagine a world in which there was no music. Whether your taste is Bach or Beethoven, punk, reggae, or New Wave, it remains true that so much joy and pleasure come from music.

However, there is something else to say here. A lot of modern music has got very angry, because in other areas of life our youthful composers find no answers and music itself, by itself, leaves the big questions unanswered. One song simply invites listeners to 'feel the warm thrill of confusion'. So its message is one of despair. In a nutshell, much modern music reflects the deep heartfelt cry of young people saying, 'Hey, world. What's it all about, man? We're confused. And so are our folks. And we're angry with all those hypocrites who give us easy answers.'

So where has modern music got us? It has got us nowhere. It has only questions, good ones, to be sure, but no answers. In consequence, it will shout itself hoarse and finally sink into silence, only to be replaced by another style for another day.

SEXUALITY

Getting back to Solomon, we see he tried not only music. He tried also the option of sex. He put it succinctly, 'Then there were my many beautiful concubines' (2:8).

However, this didn't meet his inner needs or provide answers to the questions of his quest.

Probably no previous civilisation has so explored the mechanics and psychology of sex as ours and then ended up so thoroughly perplexed and disillusioned on both the subject and the experience of it.

One of the chief proponents of the modern sexual revolution is Hugh Hefner of the multi-million-dollar success story called *Playboy*. Way back in February 1963, Hefner penned this paean of praise for permissiveness:

America has come alive again. And with the social revolution has come a sexual revolution as well. Gone is much of the puritan prudishness and hypocrisy of the past. But far from being representative of a moral decline, as some would like us to believe, we are in the process of acquiring a new moral maturity and honesty in which man's body, mind and soul are in harmony rather than in conflict.[1]

However, one year later *Time* magazine, which is hardly a Sunday school journal, wrote in an essay: 'When sex is pursued only for pleasure, or only for gain, or even only to fill a void in society or in the soul, it becomes elusive, impersonal, and ultimately disappointing.'[2] The very next year (1965) in another essay it spoke of 'the pornography of nausea' and of the 'pathetic fallacy according to which all existence revolves around sex.'[3] Hefner's revolution was not producing ecstasy, but nausea.

One New York therapist said recently: 'People are disillusioned with free sex.' This loose way hasn't brought sexual joy and fulfilment. Only a sense of dust and ashes. And more emptiness.

William Masters and Virginia Johnson, two of the most prominent sexologists of our time, did a study on all the current sexual practices in the USA today. They studied the patterns of pre-marital sex, extra-marital sex, gay sex, swinging sex (multiple couples in a sort of free-for-all), traditional marriage sex, second marriage sex – second marriage being as the celebrated Dr John once said, 'the triumph of hope over experience'!

It is instructive that though Masters and Johnson have no religious axes to grind, they end up, literally with their final paragraph, affirming that commitment to one partner for life is the best way, not simply for the society as a whole, but for the long-term sexual fulfilment of the couple themselves.

Basically they end up saying that even looked at scientifically and pragmatically and non-religiously, the

Christian view of marriage and sex is the soundest. Beyond that it doesn't suffer from having to carry the impossible emotional and spiritual weight of being explored and embraced as the basic answer to what life and the universe are all about. Solomon tried that, man down the ages has tried it, and twentieth-century with-it moderns have tried it, but all to no avail.

Solomon tried yet another area – that of intellectual pursuits.

THE MIND

Perhaps even more than we think of Solomon as a wealthy ladies' man, we think of him as a 'wise guy'. We know he was smart, a student, a scholar and an author of famous sayings. Let him speak for himself:

> Now I began a study of the comparative virtues of wisdom and folly, and anyone else would come to the same conclusion I did – that wisdom is of more value than foolishness, just as light is better than darkness; for the wise man sees, while the fool is blind. And yet I noticed that there was one thing that happened to wise and foolish alike – just as the fool will die, so will I. So of what value is all my wisdom? Then I realised that even wisdom is futile. For the wise and fool both die, and in the days to come will be forgotten. So now I hate life because it is all irrational: all is foolishness, chasing the wind (Eccles. 2:12–17).[4]

I remember, as an undergraduate headed for school-mastering, suddenly saying to myself: 'Now so what if I produce a rash of schoolboys who can read Caesar's *Gallic Wars* and talk French like a Parisian!' It would have been a noble schoolmasterly dream. But, I mean, so what? If that's all, and there's nothing else, it doesn't add up to much, does it? Thus one modern writer in a penetrating study of the meaning of life entitled *To Be or Not to Be* can have a chapter entitled 'Education for What?' In it he observes that 'education has for the time being lost its significance.'[5]

Perhaps that is because we want head-knowledge or expertise or skill to fill that aching void in the human soul, but it hasn't done so.

However educated we are, however much our mighty or not-so-mighty minds are put to work, yet that ache and void remain.

So perhaps we land up with Solomon saying, 'I hate life because it is all so irrational.'[6] 'I hated all my toil.'[7] 'I gave my heart to despair.'[8]

Or else we settle for eat, drink and be merry, for tomorrow we die.

Either way we are left without answers. Life remains a cosmic farce – or as Shakespeare's Macbeth put it, 'A tale told by an idiot, full of sound and fury and signifying nothing.'

ABSURD

I remember some years ago in London, being invited along with my wife to attend a ballet. Our gracious hosts obviously thought these country bumpkins from darkest Africa needed some cultural beefing up! So off we went for our night out.

As the curtain opened we were confronted with a stage-set consisting of a very tall pile of garden chairs on one side, as if stacked from some garden party the previous day, plus a running tap on the other. Then the musical score opened, not with any lyrical cascade of strings but with the weirdest cacophony of discordant sound you ever heard!

Next came the dancers, dressed in the weirdest outfits and contorting grotesquely around like a bevy of geese with rigor mortis.

I thought, 'Well, this is just one eccentric little cameo before the real programme gets under way.' But not a bit of it. The whole show gyrated along this bizarre path for the next several hours. And nothing but those chairs and that miserable tap for the stage-set!

'Darkest England,' I mumbled to myself. 'Give me Africa every time!'

As we walked out my thoroughly perplexed wife asked me: 'Why didn't that say anything? It was just absurd.'

'Ah!' I replied like the wise old owl. 'That's just what it did say – and said profoundly – it said life is absurd.'

And, as many modern playwrights and songsters see – that's the logical conclusion if God is dead. But is He?

STRANGE THINGS

Curiously, in the midst of all this we experience some very strange things which disturb this picture of gloom, pessimism and despondency.

First of all, we can see that there is something here – a universe, a world and planets and stars and sun and order and so on – as against there being nothing there! Secondly we humans, curious and wondrous creatures that we are, are also here, as against not being here. Are we the random products of an accident out there in empty, godless, impersonal space? Or what? Thirdly, we keep hearing of or meeting people who do rather emphatically affirm that they not only believe God exists, but have come to know Him personally in Jesus Christ, that ever-so-strange stranger of Galilee.

More baffling still are His supposed claims in the Bible not only to be a real historical figure but to be God in the flesh. So weird does the whole thing sound at first blush that we would want to consign it all to the world of fairies, hobgoblins and foul fiends, but for the fact that so many seemingly sensible, normal and intelligent people believe it so seriously. More than that it affects them so positively. Like Mitty, the taxi-driver, they've found life with a capital L!

But why do they believe this way, you ask. What makes them think God exists. More pointedly still, what makes them so sure Jesus is the Way, the Truth and the Life? And if He is, then how can He be found?

How and where we end up all depends on whether God is dead and atheism true, or whether atheism is false and God is very much alive and well. And what if our space-ship earth is indeed God's uniquely endowed and personally invaded planet?

It's quite a thought. What are we to say?

Why believe? Why affirm He lives?

Let me start with my own subjective experience, plus that of others and then move to the more objective data and evidence around us. Some of this may sound very strange and odd to you, but hang in there, and you may yet be wonderfully persuaded. Beyond that, you may even, like C. S. Lewis, the great Oxford scholar, be *Surprised by Joy*.

Chapter Three

PERSONAL ENCOUNTER

I believe Jesus Christ has verified Himself in my
experience and He can do so in yours.
Cambridge physicist, Alex Wood

A test pilot was once trying to tell an aircraft designer that
God was alive and had come into his heart in Christ. A
vigorous exchange between new-found faith and old-time
scepticism followed.

Finally the pilot put this penetrating question: 'Frank,
what argument do you have for a changed life?' The
designer had no reply.

Likewise a Salvation Army lassie was once asked how
she knew God was alive and had come into her heart in
Christ: 'Because I was there when it happened,' came the
quick retort!

Now I can say the same sort of thing. Of course I know a
sceptical reader might say, 'It's all subjective and you can't
trust subjective experience.' But let me tell you anyway
and you make up your own mind. You see, conviction of
the truth of a thing arrives when objective facts and
subjective experience come together.

David, the Psalmist in the Old Testament, put it
succinctly, 'O, taste and see that the Lord is good!'

Now it is this sort of process that I and a myriad others
have been through spiritually. That's why I feel em-
boldened to share some of these subjective experiences

first, before asking you to check them out for rationality
and reasonableness against a wide range of objective facts
and evidence.

FAITH

So let me tell you how I came to faith. I guess it started with
my mother and father raising me in a church-going home.
Not that I was turned into any angel of light thereby. In
fact Sunday school appealed to me first because I got
threepence for the collection which I then spent on
liquorice at the local café. Secondly they issued little
stamps if you attended and a full book of stamps won you
an attendance prize. Thirdly I went because it was such
fun baiting the teacher and teasing the girls. I once linked
the gorgeous blond plaits of some mummy's darling
round the pew during the teacher's talk and was delighted
out of my boots at the almost dislocated neck which
resulted when the little sweetie stood up to sing the closing
hymn!

The result of all this was that I spent most of the Sunday
school classes in the empty side of the church known as
'the disgrace pew'. Anyway, the apparently required
posture of 'eyes closed' during prayers struck me as an
enormous boon as it enabled me to return to my proper
seat unobserved until the end of the prayer. Then all those
angelic little faces, plus the teacher's exasperated
demeanour, would be rewarded with the spectacle of
Michael in living colour back in his own seat, as their
devotions ended. The teacher finally gave up and, the
attendance prize notwithstanding, consigned me to outer
darkness.

High School in an Anglican Church school found me
not appreciably reformed. My friends viewed me as a
professional prankster, a non-stop mischief-maker, a
highly skilled master-baiter, an accomplished liar, a
capable shop-lifter, and an inexplicably Holy Joe when it

came to chapel. For some reason I would attend even the voluntary services. When it came to Confirmation I demonstrated to myself, to God and to my friends my deepest seriousness by putting a full two shillings in the collection instead of the normal High School sixpence. Thus did I perplex not only myself, but others. At another level, however, I was touched, impressed and convinced by my mother that Christian morality, especially in terms of sex ethics, was the right way to go. That was something very important to me. And I saw in her and Dad a stirring and powerful example of integrity in all things financial and behavioural. Their abstemiousness also struck me and I was never tempted into the drinking scene with its intoxicating consequences.

So *something* was going on in my heart. On the one hand I knew guilt for my crimes and sins, and I felt admiration for my mother's and father's standards. I also knew moments of wonder and worship in a great hymn. It seemed there must be someone or something out there (it didn't all just happen), and I knew that certain things like kindness and fair play were better than cruelty and injustice. More than that, when in real trouble or need I called on whoever was out there. And often I seemed to be helped. It seemed I was being wooed, courted, encouraged towards a power beyond.

All this led me, in spite of some deep agnosticism within, to keep going to church. And in this frame I finally arrived at university in England.

It wasn't long before some very eager young men got their clutches on me and began to tell me of this marvellous person, Jesus Christ, whom it was possible to know in a personal way. The idea struck me as incredible, though fascinating. I mean, wasn't church attendance all that could be expected of anybody, and wasn't some sort of wobbly conviction that there was a God out there about all one could hope to achieve this side of the grave?

A beautiful early Sunday morning in October 1955 found me accompanying my friend, Robert Footner, to church at his invitation. We went to Cambridge's famous Round Church, built in Norman times in circular design. The service over, we returned to St Catharine's college to await the breakfast offering from the college kitchen. Having twenty minutes to kill, Robert invited me up to his rooms.

As he closed the door he asked out of the blue: 'Michael, do you know Christ?' Good job the door was shut or I'd have bolted. I stammered something about having gone to church all my life but Robert seemed curiously un-impressed.

Observing my bewildered look, he launched into an explanation that there was a difference between knowing God and knowing about Him, as there was between knowing the Queen of England and knowing about her.

Later, of course, I was to read John 17:3 where Jesus, in conversation with His Father, says, 'This is eternal life, that they KNOW thee, the only true God, and Jesus Christ whom thou hast sent.' This ties up with Solomon's realisation already mentioned, 'thou hast put eternity in man's heart' (Eccles.3:11). The sense of need which we all feel for an eternal dimension, is to be met, says the Bible, by the eternal life which is in Jesus Christ and in knowing Him.

The whole idea struck me back in 1955 as totally incredible. 'You mean one can actually know God personally?' It seemed too much to credit.

SURRENDER

Having delivered a left to the solar plexus, Robert now sent a right to the jaw. 'Michael, have you ever surrendered your life to Christ?' he asked. My anger and embarrass-ment at the first question having subsided to some degree, I was more rational and honest with myself about the second. Deep down I found myself recognising that I had done everything possible in the religious life, but not that.

I had never surrendered my will to Jesus Christ.

I recollect an almost elemental battle in my soul between the desire to keep going my way and the call to go Christ's. I wanted to run my life. He wanted me to surrender to Him.

I also recollect another thought. If all this was not true, I had nothing to lose. After all, if there was nothing out there, and if behind the universe, there stood only the impersonal godless and empty recesses of time and chance and accident, then, in calling on a non-existent reality, nothing would happen and life would go on unchanged. Certainly there was nothing to lose if it was all a figment of the imagination.

But suppose, just suppose, there really was something or someone there; and suppose, just suppose, Jesus actually is for real, then in calling Him into my life and surrendering myself to Him, I had everything to gain.

Nothing to lose. Everything to gain. If not true, I could carry on as usual. But if true, I would find the key to the universe.

Midstream in these mighty meanderings of mind, Robert said, 'Let me explain to you a wonderful little promise in the last book of the Bible – it's in Revelation, chapter three at verse twenty.'

Somewhere, sometime, long ago, I had heard it. Now as he read it and explained it, it hit me with the force of an express train. Here is this Jesus, putting Himself on the line and challenging me to put Him to the test. He was inviting me to use what the scientists call the 'empirical method'. That is the method of putting something to the test by the processes of trial and error. You see if a thing works.

This is what Jesus says: 'Behold I stand at the door and knock. If anyone hears my voice and opens the door, I will come in.'

Mind-boggling. Breathtaking. Incredible. He says, 'You do your part. I'll do mine. I'm knocking at the door of your heart. If you hear my inner whisper, if you feel me drawing you to myself, then do your bit and open the door and I will, I promise you, come into your heart.'

'Could it be?' I thought to myself. 'Could it really be that this One who claims to be behind all reality actually says He will enter my heart if I open the door to Him?'

In a flash I decided. I would give it a go. I would say, 'Yes'. I would yield all. Or at least I would give as much of myself as I then could to as much of God as I then understood. I couldn't do more. I shouldn't do less.

And so in a little bed-sitter on the third floor of a student residence in Cambridge, I knelt, somewhat awkwardly and slightly embarrassed, and said Yes to Jesus Christ. It was the simplest, most momentous act in which I would ever engage in either time or eternity.

PRESENCE AND PEACE

To my still somewhat perplexed and tentative eye, Robert looked absurdly and incongruously joyful as we rose from our knees.

'Well, we'll see,' said the sceptical part of me as we made our way to breakfast, having well and truly killed eighteen of the twenty minutes we had had in hand before the dining-hall opened.

After breakfast I recollect walking across the college quadrangle and looking up into the heavens. 'Well, God,' said the non-sceptical part of me, 'if you're really out there I want you to see I've done my part of the deal. Now I expect you to make yourself known to me and to do your part. Otherwise I'm all through with this thing.'

It was a bold challenge. I daren't say if I was right or wrong to make it. But I did.

The morning slipped its way through my student fingers with nothing to report. Then suddenly, midway through the afternoon, I became aware of a presence in my life – a new presence – a presence from beyond. Quite quiet, but inescapable. Real. Gripping. Overwhelming. It was God. It was Jesus. It was true!

Yes, He was there. And I knew Him. Unbelievably I was meeting Him. And He was making Himself known to me. I remembered Robert's question. 'Do you know Jesus?' It had baffled me. Now I understood. He could indeed be known. And I was in the flush of a new encounter. A bit like when a man meets that special girl for him – and knows this is it. All is luminous with the light of love and the mystery of meeting.

That night there was a student service in the Holy Trinity Church, Cambridge. Every word took meaning. I especially remember the blessing. For the first time ever it was understood. 'The peace of God, *which passes all understanding*, keep your hearts and minds in Christ Jesus. And the blessing of God the Father, God the Son and God the Holy Spirit be with you always.'

The peace which passes all understanding. That was it. As if suddenly the last piece of the jigsaw puzzle of life and the universe had fallen into place.

Oh! It was exhilarating. I jumped on my dilapidated bicycle and rushed round to an old school-friend in another college. He looked thoroughly mystified. 'You know,' he said, 'just this morning someone else in the college shared a similar story with me. There must be something in this.'

NEWNESS

For me there was no doubt about it at that point. Particularly amazing to me was the sense of newness in everything.

The next week raced by with my attitudes to parents, family, South Africa, my work, career and future all undergoing some sort of change. Beyond that Nature seemed in a new way to have the signature of God writ large across it.

The following Sunday I went to church again. Outside

the church I saw a big billboard. On it was the text, 'If any man be in Christ, he is a new creature. Old things are passed away. Behold all things are become new!'[9]

I was staggered. The verse articulated exactly my experience of the previous week. All things were becoming new. And to find and realise that this was really what the New Testament was about was heady stuff indeed. 'Goodness, even St Paul found what I've found,' I said to myself. I'd always thought Christianity was a matter of constantly turning over a new leaf. Now I saw it was receiving new life. Christianity was not a religion. It was a relationship. A relationship with the living God in Jesus Christ.

As I pull out my diaries from that period it is abundantly clear that something of mighty moment had happened in my life.

Three months after that memorable October morning I wrote in my journal, 'How tremendous it is to feel this peace and power!' (Tuesday, January 24th, 1956.) I added: 'It's funny the difference the Lord makes even to work.' The day after that: 'The Lord becomes more real day by day.' On Friday that week I penned a little prayer: 'Lord, never leave me. Always be with me like this.'

Then a sombre note on Monday, March 5th, 1956, 'Work a little depressing. Gamma plus for my essay! I must rely on the Lord for strength in my work. I will never get through this exam on my own steam. But through Christ I can do all things.'

Poor old Lord! He had to spend a lot of time bailing me out on that work – but He did!

My point in narrating this is to underline that never before had I ever thought, or written, or spoken in these categories. Clearly something very real had happened.

'It's all emotion,' said a sceptical fellow-student who was a budding young lawyer. 'I'll see you in a year's time and it will all be gone.'

A year later, on the anniversary of my commitment to Christ, I saw him.

'It's still going strong,' I called to him across the college quad.

'What a nut!' he probably thought.

And just to rub a little more salt in the wounds of his scepticism, I repeated the performance with him the following year as well!

Now, many years later, if I saw him again, I could still say, 'It's going strong.' Or else I could echo the old hymn writer: 'You ask me how I know He lives: He lives within my heart.'

Perhaps it's simplest just to affirm with Dr Alex Wood, the Cambridge physicist, 'I believe Jesus Christ has verified himself in my experience and he can do so in yours.'

Chapter Four

FROM DESPERATION TO DISCOVERY

At the foot of the cross is common ground for all men to discover God.

Bishop Festo Kivengere of Uganda

Let's change the scenario and step across seas and desert and jungle into Africa's Zimbabwe – about as far a cry from the rarefied halls of Cambridge as one could imagine.

Here is a story out of Black Africa which I want to present. As Africa is my context and I am a white African, why not let you hear a different but complementary story, from a black African who, as it happens, is also a friend and colleague. The same ingredients of spiritual enquiry and glorious discovery are present, though in Stephen's case there was a massive dislocation of life. If my sins and problems were more those of the Pharisaical elder brother in the prodigal son story of Luke 15, then Stephen's were those of the prodigal himself!

Life had been pretty tough for young Stephen. Mother and father Lungu were having a difficult time of it and finally divorced when Stephen and his brothers and sisters were quite small. What made it all worse was that neither of the parents wanted the children, who therefore felt totally rejected. Stephen put it this way:

All I knew was beatings every day and that I had to feed myself somehow. I never experienced the love of father or mother. I also denied the existence of God; I thought Jesus Christ was a white man; and if there was a God, I hated Him for bringing me into this world. I hated myself and I hated the frightening tomorrow. I said to myself, 'The only way is to end my life.' The fact is I didn't want to wake up next day and face more suffering. So one day I took a rope and tried to hang myself, but somehow didn't succeed properly. People later found me and saved my life.

Ongoing hatred built up in young Stephen till the day came when he vowed that if he saw his father or mother he would kill them. For years he stayed in the same city as his parents. It was called Harare and it was at that time a black appendage to the white city of Salisbury. The white city has now taken the name of the former township and become the capital of independent Zimbabwe.

However, although Stephen knew his parents were in the same township he never dared to see either of them for fear of what he might do to them.

DELINQUENCE

Over the following years he began taking drugs, glue, spirits and everything you care to name. He joined a gang of young thugs who used to roam the streets at night stripping and robbing people or breaking into houses in major exploits of theft.

Periodically he got some employment but the money was never enough and so he began to secure money in a variety of devious ways.

But none of this satisfied. Confessed Stephen: 'There was always a vacuum and an emptiness in my life. I tried to fill it with girls, with drink, with cigarettes, with flashy clothes and all sorts of things, but still the emptiness was there.'

This emptiness drove him to more and more desperate

activities and enterprises. One day when he was drunk and drugged he took a knife and set off to find his mother. Murder was in his heart and his hands were shaking with the resolution that was in his will. He finally found his mother and said to her, 'You must die because of the suffering you have caused me.'

His mother, pathetically worn out with the lostness of her own life, said, 'All right, son, go ahead. I am tired of this life anyway. Kill me.'

Stephen threw the knife at his mother, but mercifully for both him and her it missed her by inches. At least he did not have murder on his conscience.

But his murderous thoughts continued to press in on him. One day he accordingly set off to town to buy a new knife. Some failure of resolution held him back from committing the crime personally. So he tried to hire some other young thugs for the awful job and offered them a sum of $200, saying, 'If you will kill my mother, I will give you this money.'

To this day he does not know what prevented those young men from taking the money and carrying out the dastardly crime.

POLITICS

This sort of lifestyle held Stephen for a long time in its terrible and strangulating grip. However, a modest measure of reprieve from that dark world came with the emergence of some political light on the black man's horizon in the formerly white controlled Rhodesia. Blacks wanted independence and freedom and were determined to get it. Many were committed to doing this peacefully and democratically, but not Stephen. That way was too long, tortuous and drawn out. Rather for him the way of violence.

So he got caught up in all kinds of programmes which encouraged violence, terrorism, and the use of petrol bombs.

Now he was a young political activist with a cause. The other things he had been involved in had not brought any kind of life, peace or meaning to him, perhaps now he could find some significance in embracing a great political cause.

But the more he terrorised and the more he shouted and screamed his frustrations at the white government, the more miserable became his soul and spirit inside. The intoxication of being caught up in a great political cause quickly wore off and his soul was more shattered, drained and empty than ever before.

One Saturday afternoon he and some of his friends were walking in the streets of Harare, all armed with their petrol bombs and knives, when they saw a large tent. They heard the beating of drums and the singing of songs. They looked inside. Over a thousand people were there.

Stephen was angered and appalled to see a white man in there preaching about the power of Jesus Christ. He shouted, 'Shut up! We don't want to hear about Jesus! There is no God! There is no Jesus! Jesus is a white man!'

A couple of black clergy came up to him and pleaded with him to keep quiet.

'If you tell me to keep quiet, I'll fix you!' spat back the angry young man.

The young white preacher continued speaking. When he had finished, an African woman and another young lad stood up and shared their own experiences of coming to a discovery of Jesus Christ. Stephen calmed down a little as he listened to these sincere personal stories which seemed to have a ring of truth and reality to them. Could this all be so? Was there any truth in this? Surely, there couldn't be. It was all a bunch of rubbish. The momentarily thoughtful young man became angry again. Then his anger subsided as an African evangelist stepped up to the lectern.

SOME WILL DIE

Perhaps it is best to let Stephen share what happened next in his own words.

The African evangelist opened to Romans 6:23 and read, 'The wages of sin is death, but the gift of God is eternal life through Jesus Christ our Lord.' Then he kept quiet and looked at us. Tears were running down his face and he was quiet for what seemed like ten minutes. I had never seen such a thing. He tried to say something but his voice choked. Finally he managed to say, 'I am crying because some of you tonight are going to die. Tonight someone here is going to die. And you do not know Christ.'

Stephen recalls the experience as if it were yesterday.

When he said it the third time, I was trembling. As he went on expounding the Word of God, it was as if God Himself was speaking through him and pointing directly into my heart. I felt I was the only sinner in the whole congregation and I was restless under the conviction of the Holy Spirit. He mentioned all kinds of sins, saying, 'Murderers will not enter the Kingdom of God.' I saw myself as the vilest sinner. The Spirit of God was speaking. I was weeping like a little child. Then something strange began to happen in my heart. Next thing I found myself getting up before this preacher ended his message. I started making my way forward and I knelt down in front of the pulpit.

As the young rebel knelt there in front of the pulpit, he felt in his heart a tremendous sense of conviction that he needed Jesus Christ. There was suddenly an enormous explosion at the back of the tent. A petrol bomb had been thrown and had exploded. Pandemonium began to reign as the tent caught fire. People began running out in panic and hooligan elements began to throw stones in random fury. The chaos was complete. All hell seemed to have been let loose.

But Stephen just kept kneeling at the base of that pulpit with the chaos, confusion, and bedlam all round him. And amid the stones, the fire, the panic, the screaming (and, as he was later to discover, the death), Stephen wept his way through into repentance, faith and the most glorious spiritual discovery. 'I knew that if I did not settle the matter there and then, regardless of what was going on around me, I would perhaps never make life's greatest decision and discover Jesus Christ,' confessed Stephen later.

The transaction and commitment complete, Stephen moved from that sacred place to the back of the tent and on outside. Imagine his horror when he found out that the friend with whom he had come was dead. So was another close companion. Truly and incredibly the preacher had been right. He had wept but minutes before because the Spirit of God had shown him that some would die in that tent that night without entering a living discovery of Christ.

NEW LIFE

Looking back on that experience of 1962 the Stephen of today can write: 'That night I knelt down and confessed all my sins to Jesus Christ. I asked the King of Kings to come into my life. He took me over, and destroyed the power of cigarettes, the power of hatred, and the power of lustful passion.'

It was a chastened, humbled, but overwhelmed young man who that night walked away from the burning tent in Harare township. The first thing he did was to seek out his mother. When she saw him she drew back terrified.

'Mother, Stephen is dead,' said the young man.

'What do you mean?' she said. 'You're talking to me.'

'No, this Stephen you see before you, Mother, is a brand-new Stephen. The old Stephen is dead. Something has happened in my life, Mother, and I want to tell you about it. And I want you to forgive me because you know I wanted to kill you. But Christ has come into my heart and I am a changed person.'

Mrs Lungu was absolutely staggered. She couldn't believe what she was either seeing or hearing. Her first conclusion was an echo of one reached on the day of Pentecost twenty centuries ago. At that time when people

heard the Apostles preach they said to them, 'You are filled
with new wine. You must be drunk' (Acts 2:12–13).

Now, twenty centuries later, Mrs Lungu said to her son,
'You must be drunk. Go into the room and sleep.'

Sleep came quickly and easily to Stephen. But at 4 a.m.
he was awake. He knelt down beside his bed and said,
'Thank you Jesus for saving me.'

WITNESS

Often when people come into this new experience of
Christ, they find themselves irrepressibly constrained to
share the great discovery. Saul of Tarsus stomped the
Roman world and got the message into the very courts of
Nero. In the fourth century the once reprobate Augustine
entered the Church to become one of its greatest ever
writers and preachers. Martin Luther exploded into
sixteenth-century Europe in the mightiest mass movement of Bible translation and evangelism ever known up
to that time. In the 1800s John Wesley rode some 250,000
miles on horseback from place to place sharing the great
discovery of Jesus Christ. The modern C S Lewis of
Oxford rushed for his pen and then for a studio in the
BBC.

Stephen Lungu fell into this tradition. Next morning
going into the city-centre on a bus he stood up and said,
'Ladies and gentlemen, I want to tell you that Jesus Christ
has changed my life.'

'This is Monday. Don't preach on Monday,' the people
shouted as they pushed him out of the bus. So he got into
the next bus which arrived and began to preach again!
Said Stephen, 'I wanted to tell the whole world about this
wonderful Saviour.'

Later he found himself entering the mission organisation in whose burning tent he had come to a knowledge
of Christ some years previously.

Some seven years after his own commitment to Christ

Stephen was preaching one day in a market-place and found himself counselling a number of enquirers who had responded to his message. To his wonder, astonishment and gratitude, one of these turned out to be the mother he had tried to kill. He then had the glorious privilege of leading her into the discovery of Christ. She too became a brand-new person and to this day she has meetings for children and for women wherever she goes.

In 1980 I met Stephen Lungu in Malawi and our hearts were curiously drawn and knitted together. I began to wonder whether perhaps he was not called to share with us in our own Christian ministry in African Enterprise, the mission organisation with which I am associated.

'God has already called me to work with you, Mike,' responded Stephen with a radiant smile! And thus has it worked out.

Well, there we are. I came from religious Pharisaism to discovery. Lungu came from desperation and delinquence to discovery.

Discovery? Discovery of what? Discovery of the living God in the face and person of Jesus Christ. This I most truly believe. Beyond that, I hope and pray most earnestly that this will be your discovery too, if you have never made it, before you have finished the pages of this book.

Chapter Five

FAITH AND DOUBT

Unless I see in His hands the print of the nails and place
my finger in the mark of the nails, and place my hand in
His side, I will not believe.
Thomas – John 20:25

Like Thomas in the New Testament, you have now heard
a couple of stories about Jesus and His impact on several
people's lives. But perhaps, also like him, you still have a
real battle to believe. The stories you hear make you feel
deep down that conceivably there is something in it all,
but you yourself just can't quite get into it or accept it. And
you don't want to be rushed. You'd like to see the wood for
the trees, but frankly you can't.

That's fine. Don't panic. Let's just get down to a bit of
jungle clearing.

UNBELIEF

First of all, let's make a distinction between doubt and
unbelief. In my understanding, doubt is a problem of the
mind which wants to believe but can't. With this, Jesus
and the New Testament have real sympathy.

By contrast, unbelief is a problem of the will which
could believe, but won't. The Bible sees this as sin. It is the

problem of the person who is quite unwilling to follow the facts where they lead because he or she is unwilling to make the moral changes of lifestyle to which such a pursuit of truth might lead.

I remember during a university mission meeting up with a delightful young man who professed many intellectual problems about Christianity. We discussed these at length and then agreed to talk again following a game of squash planned for a few days later.

Armed with my racket, ball and lots of energy, I arrived at my young friend's rooms on campus en route to the courts. I knocked, but received no reply. So I entered the room to await his arrival.

What met me was one of the most interesting species of wallpapering I have ever seen. In a nutshell the walls and ceiling were a living-colour display of the bare facts. In fact, the nudes on the ceiling were at least life-size and more than beckoning. I realised that all this would be somewhat distracting from meaningful spiritual discussion! Anyway, my friend never showed up, so the discussion never happened. I suspect he was fleeing from facing Christ more than from being beaten at squash!

So what could I conclude but that my young sceptic's problems were much more moral than they were intellectual? He was not a doubter, but an unbeliever. He wanted Jesus Christ as much as burglars want policemen or mice want the cat. He was not in search. He was in flight.

Said Jesus of such people: 'Neither will they be persuaded, though one rose from the dead.'[10] In other words, no amount of well-presented or persuasive evidence will convince such a person. *They don't want to believe, because they don't want to change.* The intellectual problems they profess are only fig-leaves to hide the nakedness of their moral and spiritual rebellion.

The hard fact is that a willingness to obey God and follow Christ is a prerequisite of spiritual discovery. Jesus put it this way: 'If any of you really determines to do God's

will, then you will certainly know whether my teaching is
from God.'[11]

Now I doubt whether any reader who has got this far in
these pages is likely to be in the 'unbeliever' category. But
to grasp this distinction between doubt and unbelief is
very important. While we must be on guard against
wishful thinking we must just as truly guard against
wishful unthinking!

DOUBT

Now, what of the doubter? If you are such, then perhaps
your problem is based on a real wondering as to whether
this is all true. Maybe you feel like the schoolboy who
defined faith as 'believing in something which you know
isn't true!'

A number of years ago now a spirited conversation took
place between Henry Ward Beecher, who was a prominent
New York pastor, and Thomas Ingersole, the philo-
sophical sceptic.

Said Beecher wryly: 'You know, Ingersole, you philo-
sophers are like a blind man stumbling round in a dark
room looking for a black cat which isn't there.'

Ingersole shot back: 'You know, Beecher, you Christians are like a blind man stumbling round in a dark room
looking for a black cat which isn't there – and you FIND
one!'

For Ingersole, Christianity was based on some sort of
fabrication – an imaginary happening long ago.

He would have identified, as perhaps some reader
might, with the Queen's reply in *Alice in Wonderland*
when poor Alice protested that 'one can't believe
impossible things'.

'I dare say, you haven't had much practice,' said the
Queen. 'When I was your age, I always did it for half an
hour a day. Why, sometimes I've believed as many as six
impossible things before breakfast.'

Now if your basic feeling is that Christianity is based on either believing in a black cat which isn't there, or believing as many as six impossible things before breakfast, then there are several vitally important points to make.

First of all, if Christianity is not true, then it's the biggest farce and fake going and its perpetration is little short of wicked. After all, to get people to deceive themselves by believing a lie or a fraud is scandalous.

Secondly, to believe against the evidence or against the facts of history is to commit intellectual suicide. No one is asking for that.

Thirdly, no one should be pushed into any form of Christian response until his or her mind is satisfied at the very least that what we are talking about would basically seem to be true.

Fourthly, be assured that doubt can in fact crumble as evidence is faced and as intellectual conviction grows. As this happens, a step of faith in Christ becomes possible.

ANYONE THERE?

Of course I realise that for numbers of twentieth-century people the religious problem starts not with faith in Christ, but with whether there is a God at all. The problem is also related to origins and where we all came from.

At this point we need to note that every human being does have some sort of belief system. We may not be very clear as to its form or shape, but it is there nevertheless. And it affects how we behave, how we spend our time, how we relate to others, how we think of the world around us, as well as what makes us happy, angry or sad.

In this we will have been affected by our heredity and upbringing, our culture and the values of the society we live in.

Realising that each of us does in fact have some sort of belief system, we then have to take it and step out with it into the real world around us and see which belief system, our own or some other presented to us, can make best sense of all the data of life which come at us.

In this we will need to recognise, as Jean Paul Sartre, the French philosopher, did, that the basic issue we all face is that something (the world, universe, and us) is 'there', as against the alternative of its not being there! I mean, *something* is there, rather than *nothing*. This is a very great mystery. It really is. What is more, there is this very odd fact that we as humans are here and able to observe it all and reflect on it.

NO GOD?

The question is whether there is a God behind it all. Now there are different answers to this. There is the answer of the atheist who dogmatically says there is no God. (Someone once defined the atheist as 'a fellow with no invisible means of support!') Be that as it may, the fact is that some affirm the whole idea of God to be a fairy tale.

While some see this sort of view as intellectually sophisticated, the Bible for its part does not share that perception. It says simply, 'the fool has said in his heart there is no God.'[12]

Suppose I drew a circle in front of you like this.

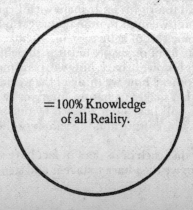

= 100% Knowledge
of all Reality.

And suppose for a moment that you are a self-styled atheist. That circle represents the sum total of all there is to know about anything. Now let me put a question to you.

'If I were to ask you how much you personally know of the sum total of all reality, what would be your reply?'

If you were a school sixth-former, you might answer 1 per cent. If so, you would be brave and bold indeed! Einstein said: 'I do not know one hundredth of 1 per cent about anything!' He also said, 'Scientists stand only on the fringe of knowledge'. That puts most of the rest of us on the fringe of the fringe of the fringe!

Anyway let's concede the sixth-former's 1 per cent for the sake of argument. Now we have another circle like this.

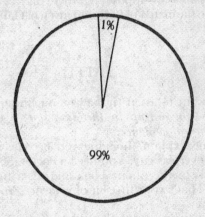

The tiny slice represents the 1 per cent of reality which you personally know about. The 99 per cent represents the rest of reality about which on your own admission you know nothing. Now we must ask: 'Could God conceivably exist within that 99 per cent of reality of which by your own admission you know nothing?'

Of course, the answer has to be 'Yes, He could.' At which point you would by definition have to cease being an atheist. You see, to be an atheist you have to know everything. You have to have a full knowledge of that 100 per cent of reality. For only on the basis of 100 per cent knowledge can you say 'I've looked at it all. I have examined it all. I understand it all. And I can tell you there is no God there.'

Only that way, can we be atheists. However, if we say, 'There *could* be a God in that 99 per cent, but I don't know for sure if there is,' then we become agnostics (tr. Latin *agnosco* = I don't know) which is far more logical and reasonable.

The question then becomes whether there is any evidence for God which could help us move from saying, 'I don't know if there is a God,' to saying 'Well, it is not *unreasonable* to suppose that there may be a God.' This gets us to the matter of faith and just what faith is and what it involves.

FAITH

Now I want to assert rightaway something very crucial. *Faith is not a leap in the dark, but a trusting in a sufficiency of evidence.*

Let me explain. Imagine you become sick in some strange overseas city. You need a doctor. So you look up 'Medical' in the phone book and see a list of doctors' names. That's your first bit of evidence. You select Dr A Jones.

Then you proceed to the address listed. Lo and behold, you find an office marked with a handsome plaque on the door – *Dr A Jones MD*. There's your next bit of evidence.

You enter, and find yourself in a waiting-room manned by a receptionist in a white dress and wearing a little upside-down watch on her lapel. You explain yourself and your sore side and she kindly asks you to wait till Dr Jones can see you. More positive evidence. It all looks pretty good so far.

You sit down on the 1930-vintage couch and reach into the pile of magazines. Sure enough – more evidence as you survey a stack of *Time* magazines going back to 1931 plus *Ladies' Home Journals* from the year dot. When you see these resting in the shadow of a plastic daisy, you know this has all got to be for real. A doctor is housed here, for sure!

Soon you are ushered into the inner sanctum. No one is there at first, but you are much reassured by the high observation bed, the big desk and the framed degree certificate in Latin (authenticity writ large) which says something about Alphonso Jones, MD Universitas Edinburghensi, or something. The evidence is now piling up. It all points too much one way to be anything other than a solid basis for you to make an act of faith in the said Dr Jones!

Finally, a friendly, clean-shaven gentleman enters wearing a white coat, dangling a stethoscope round his neck and smelling of Dettol. You are home and dry. This is it. As much evidence as you need is in – i.e. a sufficiency of evidence is there. But note. You do not have exact and precise scientific proof that the whole thing is not a hoax from start (i.e. the phone-book entry) to finish (i.e. the white coat, stethoscope and smell of Dettol!)

However, all the probabilities point so overwhelmingly in one direction that you feel ready, without committing any intellectual suicide, to tell the doctor your problem, listen to his diagnosis, and then allow him to take your appendix out.

Of course, once the operation is over and done with and the appendix plus previous pain is gone, you can tell others that your faith in the good Dr Jones was well placed and thoroughly vindicated. You are now a confirmed believer in Dr Jones!

So it is with Christian faith. We have to face the problems in the way of faith, weigh up the evidences in favour of faith, and then, if persuaded, take a step of trusting the object of faith and committing ourselves to it.

In this process of quest we shall of course need a real humility of mind. Perhaps you could pray a prayer something along these lines: 'O God, if you are really there, please help me to understand what this faith thing is all about. Help me as I face my intellectual difficulties and let the jungle undergrowth of my confusion give way to clarity of mind and responsiveness of will as I examine the evidence presented to me. Please know that if I am persuaded I will commit myself to you and follow you all my days.'

Chapter Six

NOT A CHANCE

Marvels are many, but man is the greatest.
Sophocles 445–406BC

In the next few chapters I want to present some strands of data *and evidence* which should enable the enquirer to say, 'Yes, the Christian idea of a Creator God makes good sense.'

And this conclusion would be reached not by facing any one piece of conclusive evidence, but rather by looking at clusters of evidence relating to different pieces of the jigsaw puzzle.

One writer has put it this way:

In a murder mystery, before the murderer can be named, twelve impartial jury men have to be convinced that he is guilty. They have both to *eliminate the obvious alternatives*, including accidental death, and also to reconstruct the picture so that it makes convincing sense as a whole. *No particular piece of evidence is in itself conclusive, unless it is in the sense of being just the last point which correlates an otherwise baffling collection of apparently unconnected facts.* But the conviction comes from facing the picture as a whole. Some points are essential to the case and if they were proved false the whole case would collapse. Much depends on the clarity and conviction with which these cardinal factors are demonstrated. But even so, if we concentrate entirely on these particular items piecemeal, we shall never come to a conclusion. We have got to be willing to stand back from the detail and try to see it whole.[13]

MAN THE MACHINE

Perhaps we should pause to look at ourselves first. 'Can man as we know him possibly be accounted for without God?'

Now it is obvious that we are very extraordinary creatures to have landed here by chance. Even at the physical level the human body is a most astonishing machine.

Take the marvels of the eye and the wonders of sight. Suppose you were looking down a microscope at an amoeba. The amoeba has one cell. But the human eye which views it has some 107 million cells in only one layer of the retina, that containing the so-called rods and cones. Imagine the total number of cells in the rest of the eye!

The whole thing is so incredibly amazing that every time we see anything we should be shouting doxologies into heaven.

Or take the ear. The other night I enjoyed a Beethoven concert with our local orchestra. The sounds I heard were magnificent, yet I heard them and enjoyed them and revelled in them without really thinking or reflecting on the marvellous process involved.

Dr Paul Brand, has this to say about the ear:

Further in are individual so-called cilia (i.e. hairlike vibrating organs), comparable to the rods and cones of the eye, that transmit specific messages of sound to the brain. My brain combines these messages with other factors – how well I like classical music, how familiar I am with the piece being played, the state of my digestion, the friends I am with – and offers the combination of impulses in a form I perceive as pleasure.[14]

The whole process is a marvel of intricate wonder. How

right of the Psalmist to exult and affirm 'I am fearfully and wonderfully made'.[15]

BONES AND LIMBS

Then there is the bone phenomenon in the human body. Even though much of its strength relies on the accompanying muscles etc. around it, it remains a marvel of engineering. In fact not a single twentieth-century engineering genius has yet discovered a material as well suited for the body's needs as bone. It comprises only one fifth of the body's weight, yet gives it a frame and structure of unbelievable strength and durability.

Apparently as far back as 1867 an engineer was able to demonstrate that the arrangement of bone cells forms the lightest structure made of the least material to support the body's weight. It is now nearly 120 years later and no one has successfully challenged his findings.

Or else think of something as pedestrian (sorry!) as your feet! Have you ever stopped to reflect on the daily miracle of walking, or playing a game of soccer or doing some daily knee bends and all that is involved for your feet?

Twenty-six bones line up in each of our feet and the interplay of these bones and the stress they can absorb boggles the imagination. Perhaps next time you watch the World Cup soccer on the telly you might like to reflect that each player is subjecting each foot with its twenty-six small bones to a cumulative force of over one thousand tons during the match. Yet the bones absorb the violent stress and maintain their elasticity.

But maybe you are not a soccer player. Perhaps you walk the block. Do you know that each of us walks some 65,000 miles in his or her lifetime? Just to swell your head a little more, let me tell you that that represents a little stroll going two and a half times around the world!

That's what your feet cope with – and mostly without a blister or broken bones!

Doesn't all this highlight how much we take for granted? The trouble is that we are over-familiar with the unbelievably amazing bodies which we have so that we don't see just what evidence for the creator is present in the physical frame we inhabit.

The human heart is another astonishing phenomenon. It pumps our 10 pints of body blood many times a day throughout 60,000 miles of arteries and veins. In fact the heart, even at rest, pumps so steadily and powerfully that in a single day it pushes the 10 pints of blood in the average adult body through more than 1,000 complete circuits, thus actually pumping a total of some 12,000 pints of blood in a day. If that's what it does at rest, imagine how it steps up when we exert ourselves in exercise. How astonishing! No man ever made a pump that efficient and reliable. It contracts 4,000 times per hour and beats 100,000 times per day. Someone said that if all the heart's daily work and energy were stored and released at once, it could launch your body one mile vertically into space! Anyway, don't try it. Just note it!

MALE AND FEMALE

And what of the very presence on planet earth of the mutually complementary, mutually attractive and mutually dependent creatures called man and woman? Not only are their bodies a miracle of physical synchronisms but they are clearly designed both physically and psychologically with consummate engineering skill and precision, for joyful fusion. Is all that ultimately the consequence of some accident of molecular collision out there in the impersonal and godless wastes of outer space?

Beyond that, their souls and minds and gifts and abilities and instincts are manifestly arranged – surely by a higher power and not by a freak accident – to be fused into a unity of team work and labour so as to make life on earth joyful, satisfying, fulfilling, rewarding and manageable.

To me the male-female phenomenon is indeed a mighty and marvellous evidence for God which no one in favour of romance and joy should ever ignore. Indeed the reproductive act and processes boggle the mind for mystery and wonder. Said the writer of Ecclesiastes: 'As you do not know how the Spirit comes to the bones in the womb of a woman with child, so you do not know the work of God who makes everything.'[16]

This brings us to the most ultimate physical miracle of all – that of reproduction.

The human body grows from the fertilisation of a single egg. In his book *The Medusa and the Snail*, Lewis Thomas wonders why the world made such a fuss over the test-tube baby born in England. The really special miracle, he says, lies in the common union of a sperm and egg in a process that ultimately produces a human being: 'The mere existence of a cell,' he writes, 'should be one of the greatest astonishments of the earth. People ought to be walking around all day, all through their waking hours, calling to each other in endless wonderment, talking of nothing except that cell.'[17]

Here is why this is so incredible:

Over nine months these cells divide up their functions in exquisite ways. Billions of blood cells appear, millions of rods and cones – in all, up to one hundred million million cells form from a single fertilised ovum. And finally a baby is born, glistening with liquid. Already his cells are cooperating. His muscles limber up in jerky awkward movements; his face recoils from the harsh lights and dry air of the new environment; his lungs and vocal chords join in a first air-gulping yell.

Within that clay-coloured, wrinkled package of cells lies the miracle of the ecstasy of community. His life will include the joy of seeing his mother's approval at his first clumsy words, the discovery of his own unique talents and gifts, the fulfilment of sharing with other humans. He is many cells, but he is one organism. All of his hundred trillion cells know that.[18]

Well, I don't know about you, but to me all of this speaks volumes for the reality of a designer somewhere. I just cannot accept that it is all the result of impersonal energy plus time plus chance. There's got to be more to it than that.

CHANCE

Let's think about chance for a moment. Now, to be fair, there is theoretically just the remotest possibility that it all could have come about by chance. But how remote it is we shall see!

One wag penned this not very distinguished poetic statement:

> There once was a hairy baboon
> Who always blew down a bassoon
> For he said 'It appears
> that in billions of years –
> I shall certainly hit on a tune!'

Now I suppose we would have to say that given an infinity of time, such a possibility both of the tune and of our arriving accidentally from the impersonal, is real, though the odds are billions to one against. And as we wouldn't operate even the local race-course that way, it becomes surprising when people embrace a theory of life's origins with those odds against it.

The better known though equally frivolous hypothesis of chance is that a team of monkeys typing for an infinite period of time would sooner or later produce the complete works of Shakespeare.

One story tells of such an experiment. The monkeys had been typing for decades with no orderly statement appearing. Finally one ecstatic professor saw something emerging and rushed through to his colleagues with the typescript which read:

To be or not to be…
That is the umzinsquatch!

Oh well! You can't win all the time!

Another familiar line on the chance tack relates to the odds on a kettle freezing when put on a hot stove. It would seem to be against all laws and all odds for it to happen at all, but might it not happen just once by chance? What if you packed the universe with kettles and hot stoves? Would that improve the odds?

Well, we know the odds against it happening, even with billions of kettles on billions of stoves, would be billions to one. But just suppose it happened once, think now of the odds against it happening twice. Or of it happening several times. Beyond that, think of it happening *consistently* – which is what we face with the development of life on our planet. It's as if the dice is rolling six all the time.

But if in fact the kettle did freeze on a hot stove, would it not be better and more satisfactory to explain it supernaturally than by the hopeless odds of chance? Rather than say that Nature against all odds has defied its own laws, would it not be better to seek an explanation beyond Nature – in Supernature – i.e. in the supernatural? Once admit the probability of something beyond Nature and you can stop forcing mathematical and statistical odds to stand absurdly on their heads. You might just as well expect the Oxford English Dictionary to emerge from an explosion in a print shop or to visualise the Skylab space-craft resulting from a tornado in a junk-yard!

I'm told that Sir Frederick Hopkins, the great British biochemist, once said: 'The advent of life was the most improbable event in the history of the universe.' Astronomers Fred Hoyle and Chanora Wickramasinghe recently put the chance of a natural origin on Earth of living matter as 1 in 10 raised to the power of 40,000!

Even Professor Andrew Huxley, a physiologist and President of the Royal Society, who thought that life started with a much simpler self-replicating system than that envisaged by Hoyle, conceded that scientifically the way in which life and man started is still a wide open issue.

That being the case, we are still looking for answers, but chance, it would seem, is the least satisfactory explanation of all.

So we must explore further.

Chapter Seven

QUITE A THOUGHT

> We are so impressed by the greatness and multiplicity of
> the World we know, that we seldom reflect upon the
> amazing fact of our knowing it... But this fact of
> knowledge is more remarkable than all the varieties of
> known objects put together.
>
> Archbishop William Temple

Let's think where we've got to. We began this volume
talking about the problem of meaning. 'What's it all
about?' That's the question the world is asking. We then
advanced the Christian thesis that life has its fulfilment
and meaning in a personal discovery of Jesus Christ as
God and Saviour and we heard two stories of people who
believed that they had proved that thesis true in their
personal lives and experience.

Then we admitted that this thesis is not really
acceptable to everyone, and needs for many considerable
bolstering before they can accept it and lay their lives on
the line to test it.

So we began a backtracking process, beginning with life
and the world as we know it and then seeing what
evidences there are to confirm the reality of a personal
power beyond man which we'll call God. Now, we haven't
yet got to Jesus Christ and the evidence around Him. We
are still looking at some of the data from the world of
ourselves and the universe around us to see if the pointers

there suggest the existence of God or not. This led us to reflect on a major piece of evidence which is we ourselves – Man the physical Creature.

In all of this we have been using our minds, though possibly without stopping to reflect on the incredible phenomenon of the existence of mind in the first place or on the implications of its use. And it's this which I want to close in on for a while. We are to reflect not just on Man the Marvellous Machine but on Man the Thinker and Man the Moral Being.

MAN THE THINKER

Let's for the moment get back to one of the notions referred to in the last chapter, that the universe does not have a God behind it. There is no one there. It is simply the result of impersonal energy, plus time, plus chance. And we ourselves are basically rather fabulous physical machines which likewise arrived by accident somewhere along the line.

However, when we stop to think about it, and to think about the process of thinking about it, we will run into some very amazing things!

And perhaps the most amazing is the fact that we can think at all! We have something called mind and it marks us out as totally distinct from the animal and natural world around us.

Let me reiterate William Temple's marvellous observation at the head of this chapter. 'We are so impressed by the greatness and multiplicity of the world we know, that we seldom reflect upon the amazing fact of our knowing it . . . But this fact of knowledge is more remarkable than all the varieties of known objects put together.'[19]

MIND

It is indeed breathtaking that we have minds with which to

reflect and to observe and study the world. Moreover, the mind actually transcends what it studies because it can stand back from it and evaluate. The mind studies the world around it, but the world around it does not study the mind. We are thus in a sense greater than the world around us.

What is even more remarkable is that the world around us lends itself to study with our minds. When we study astronomy, or biology, or physiology or botany, we find not a chaotic, unintelligible, random, confused, meaningless set of data, but rather a body of data which all comes together in intelligible categories, laws, principles and patterns. This is astounding. It really is.

What it means is that mind is meeting mind. It is not meeting impersonal chaotic gibberish. It is meeting mind. Orderly mind.

Sir James Jeans, the great British scientist, once said: 'We discover that the universe shows evidence of a designing or controlling power that has Something in common with our individual minds.'[20]

Our minds and the world our minds study seem to be tuned in on one another, as if designed for one another by a common mind which is above and beyond them both! So it is that when we apply our minds aright to the world around us we get results which make sense to us. Remarkable, indeed.

Beyond that we find that with these minds of ours we are discovering or uncovering truths about the world. We didn't put those truths there. We just uncovered or discovered truth which had already been put there by some mind vastly greater than our own.

But if our whole existence is simply an accident – the result of impersonal energy plus time plus chance – then we cannot account for mind meeting mind as we study and observe the world around us.

More than that. We cannot account for our minds themselves. After all, how could non-mind produce mind? It would require the effect to be greater than the cause which is impossible.

MYSTERY

Now here is the mystery, as Archbishop William Temple once noted, that 'All attempts to trace in Evolution an explanation of the emergence of mind have totally failed. And if this is not explained, the Process is not explained, for this is an element in the Process.'[21]

You see, even if we accept some form of evolution in the process of origins, we are not in fact explaining origins, but only giving a label to the process. We are not saying what set the stage for the process, or what set the process going, or what keeps the process going!

So we are confronted with this astounding fact that somewhere along the line mind has emerged in or out of the evolutionary process of the universe. And if we are to explain Nature (containing mind within it), then it surely is some form of Mind which alone can explain Nature.

And as we make this assertion we see why people like Sir James Jeans could once describe the universe as 'more like a great *thought* than like a great machine.'[22]

It also brings home to us that no theory of origins will do which only explains the lowest. It must explain the highest, which is the emergence somewhere along the line of mind, morality, aesthetic appreciation and love. In other words the theory must explain man in all his uniqueness, and not just the amoeba!

This being so, it is clear that to begin with the mindless or impersonal will not give us the explanations we need.

VALUE

Now suppose we were to concede the view that we were nothing more than some sort of rather marvellous mental and physical machine dumped down without explanation in the middle of another very much larger machine.

First of all, this would give us real problems with our *value* as individuals. Man as part of the machine would be of no more value than any other part of the machine. Neither you nor I would be able to claim more value than a dog or a rock. In point of fact, chemically, we aren't worth much more than £2 on today's market. We used to be worth about £1.50, but what with inflation and all that we have gone up in price!

In that scale of values running over a chicken or a child would make little difference because value is not really a meaningful term to introduce into such a world.

Yet even the atheist places value on people and would run over a dog rather than a child if it came to a choice. But that in fact is illogical in an impersonal, godless universe. You see, the atheist or the godless man cannot live consistently with his own commitments. Strictly speaking he should either forgo his godlessness or his rationality. He can't hold both. If he remains godless he shouldn't attach any more value to himself than he would to a rock or a dog. But that is an affront to all his instincts and to all his rationality. That means that if he would hold to both his rationality and his consistency, he must then forgo his godlessness and make room for God in his thinking processes.

FREEDOM

The next problem for us if we are only magnificent mental and physical machines lies in the area of our freedom. Under what some call 'the mechanistic scheme of things' (i.e. the machine view) there can in true fact be no such thing as freedom of choice. Free will becomes nonsense. Freedom of choice is a pure illusion, because machines don't choose, they just respond. Your computer can't say to you: 'I choose not to work this afternoon because I've got a date with a typewriter!' But if we make man just a non-choosing machine with no freedom of choice, then we in fact lock him into a closed system of nature and natural law.

But you and I know how much we cling to our freedom of choice. If I were to tell you you couldn't go to this restaurant or that movie theatre or the other hotel, you would get very uptight because you would see me infringing your freedom of choice.

But where do you get this concept of the 'right to choose'? In a godless, impersonal universe you can have no such rights. The concept is meaningless.

For example, why *shouldn't* whites dominate blacks in South Africa and remove from them the freedom to choose where they will live, or eat, or go to school? Why *should* they be given an opportunity to choose their government? In a godless, impersonal universe there can be no answer to that question. In fact in such a world I can do what I like because nothing means anything, and my supposed instincts or commitments about freedom are delusions and void of consequence.

But can you really live with that? I doubt it. Deep down you know that rational freedom of choice is crucial to what it means to be a human being at all. We live in a world where being free to choose matters and in which there are creatures for whom it matters. That is very mysterious, and much more incomprehensibly so if there is nothing beyond man and the machine.

MORALITY

Of course if we do toss our free will and responsibility to choose out of the window, then there is another major casualty and that is our concept of morality. In fact there can be *no morality*, because if man is determined simply by his heredity plus his environment, then what is, is right! What's there is all there is, so what is there is OK.

In this moral area it is also intriguing that the person who says there is no god, and who affirms, let's say, that there is no such thing as sex ethics, will actually get very put out and stand on a moral high-horse if you try to steal *his* wife! He says he doesn't believe in God, but if you steal his money or crash on purpose into his car, he will rush you to court and of all things 'demand justice'! My goodness, he has a sense of morality after all. But where did he get it from? With his presuppositions about a godless, impersonal universe, I should have thought he would allow me as much right to his money, wife or car as he has. Yet he protests. Why? Is he not being inconsistent?

Perhaps this fellow will even say somewhere along the line, 'You ought not to have done that.'

What then becomes obvious with such a fellow is that although God is apparently nowhere in his frame of thinking, yet he is in fact really using God-words, religious language, we might say, when he talks about you as a 'bad guy' and how you 'ought' to do this or that or when he laments your lack of 'conscience'. Strictly those words or concepts don't belong to him. They only belong to the person with a religious view of life.

But actually our friend, deep down, knows he is caught up in some sort of *moral order*. In fact deep down, if he really stops to think about it, he knows that such a moral order is necessary if one is to have any order in the world at all!

MORAL ORDER

This is actually rather fascinating. I suppose the real question is how we got such a moral order. Did it come from a big someone out there called God, or from popular consensus, or some sort of instinct or from the majority vote of your countrymen or from some Orwellian Big Brother of government laying down the law?

Gerald Priestland, the popular BBC religious broadcaster, makes the point that basic moral values have been around for a pretty long time and the world didn't have to wait for Christianity to come along to invent them. 'They are known as "natural morality", the implication being that they are part of human nature.' He observes that almost anywhere you look, regardless of race or culture, you will find certain principles insisted upon. The telling of truth and the keeping of promises constitute two examples, while almost all societies insist upon some kind of sexual discipline, attach some value to human life, and some kind of rights to property.[23]

All this points further to the fact that there is some sort of law of right and wrong which presses in on man from beyond him. And if you are a serious enquirer after the truth you must face this and come at it, not just as a being, but as a *human being*.

And I venture to guess that if you do that, you will quickly get the evidence to convince you that marvellous machine though you may be, you are certainly not merely a machine. You are much more mysterious than that. So mysterious in fact that I doubt if you can explain yourself except as a unique creature made by God in His own image. And that's also what Genesis says.

Chapter Eight

IN THE BEGINNING GOD

Science without religion is Lame.
Religion without Science is Blind.
Albert Einstein

Coming now to the message of Genesis, there are two related and basic questions to ask. First, what does Genesis say? Secondly what does Genesis mean?

LANGUAGE

This faces us rightaway with the matter of language used in the Bible. There are several points here.

First of all, the language of the Bible as far as natural things are concerned, is popular and not scientific. It comes to us in what was for the Hebrews the language that ordinary man used in his social chitchat and in the market-place. It does not come to us in the technical terminology of twentieth-century science. If it had, no non-scientist and certainly no pre-twentieth-century people could have understood it.

Secondly, the language the Bible uses is that which sets forth the way things appear to the observations of the ordinary man. The story is told from the perspective of man upon earth as he sees things. So when the Bible says 'The sun rises and the sun goes down' (Eccles. 1:5), or when it affirms 'The world is established: it shall never be moved' (Ps. 93:1), it is not making a scientific statement but affirming how it appears to man, the ordinary observer, as against man the technical and scientific observer.

Or again when the Bible speaks of 'the four corners of the earth' (Isa. 11:12AV) it is not committing us to a 'flat-square' view of the world any more than you would commit yourself to a world neatly divided into four if you said 'people came to our conference from all quarters'.

This sort of language is neither scientific nor anti-scientific. It is just popular day-to-day talk. The Bible's language is therefore not anti-scientific but pre-scientific. It can speak as truly for its own age as for ours or for any to come.

STATEMENT AND MEANING

In the message of Genesis we find several key affirmations.

First of all, it says God is behind everything. He is the unargued cause of all else. Nor is He explained. He is simply there – as the sovereign initiator and cause of all else.

Thus the Bible says: 'In the beginning God created... and God said... and God saw... and God called... and God blessed... and God finished...'

Then, by the picture of the six successive days, Genesis 1 says God worked progressively to complete what He had begun. There was a process involved. Evolutionists agree.

This culminated in man as a unique being who is made like God – or 'in the image of God' (Gen. 1:27AV). He is godlike in having personality, rationality, free will, moral accountability and aesthetic appreciation.

Above all, he and all creation are declared to be 'very good' (Gen. 1:31).

Then in Genesis 3 comes tragedy. Man misuses his freewill – a quality he had of necessity to possess if love as the highest good in the universe was to be possible. Then comes alienation and distance both from God and from Eve, his female helpmate, given (Gen. 1:27) in the amazing mercy and goodness of God because 'it was not good for man to be alone' (Gen. 2:18) and so that the earth be peopled by human multiplication. 'Be fruitful and multiply' (Gen. 1:28).

Now we find man at loggerheads with himself and with his neighbour. Cain murders Abel in Genesis 4 and a truly ugly side to man's nature now becomes a feature of his behaviour in all subsequent history.

One wag even has the animal world in protest over what man allowed himself to become.

> Three monkeys sat in a coconut tree,
> discussing things as they're said to be.
> Said one to the others: 'Now listen
> you two, there's a certain rumour that
> can't be true –
> That man descended from our noble race;
> the very idea is a disgrace.'

The monks then catalogue all the horrible things humans do which they wouldn't. Finally they conclude:

> Here's another thing a monk won't do,
> go out at night and get in a stew
> or use a gun, or club, or knife,
> to take some other monkey's life.
> Yes, man descended, the ornery cuss,
> but, brother, he didn't descend from us!

OK, you monks, we get the point. But Genesis had it first when it revealed man becoming a wayward creature with a nature now turned away from the purposes of God. And everyone of us in the late twentieth century knows what it is to have to live with a nature exactly like that. Genesis is re-enacted every day in each of our daily lives at some level or other as we say 'God, I can get along without you.'

But the Genesis story and revelation doesn't stop with man going wrong. It shows a God who is involved and remains involved with His special creature, man, who needs rescue, guidance and moral instruction. Beyond that He is revealed as caught up with His universe which needs upholding and sustaining by His purposes and providence. Although totally supreme over space and time, God is going to see His creation through to its appointed goals and will not stand apart from His handiwork (deism) or over-identify Himself with it (pantheism). Nor will He ever forsake man, His special creation. The laws of nature, so well recognised by modern science, are to the Bible the laws of God. And, incidentally, as such, they may, if His purposes so require it, be interrupted or superseded in a given moment. That's when a miracle happens!

That's what Genesis says. Now what does evolution say and can the two find common cause in any way?

EVOLUTION

There can be no doubt that the publication of Darwin's *Origin of Species* in 1859 was a major milestone in human thought and its influence has been mighty.

In a nutshell evolutionary theory proposes that different species derived from other existing species by a process of descent which made different sorts of modification and development possible. This process of descent is supposed to run through the whole organic world, including man himself. Fossil records supposedly give sufficient grounds to accept the continuity linkage of all forms of life.

Evolutionary theory postulates a mechanism called natural selection to explain this evolving process. It suggests that in the struggle for survival experienced by all living things, those living things which are the fittest through some inherited difference from their 'fellows', will survive more readily and leave more 'offspring', as it were, than those which are less fit, less strong or less well adapted. This is the celebrated 'survival of the fittest'.

In other words millions of years ago lifeless matter, somehow acted upon by natural forces, gave origin to one or more minute living organisms which have since evolved into all living and extinct plants and animals, including man. In its wider aspects the theory of evolution embraces the origin and development of the whole universe. Beginning several billion years ago, the universe began to develop from a few elementary compounds into its present state through the simple or uniform laws of physics and chemistry. Man thus comes as the pinnacle of the process, though he may yet go on to vast and hitherto unimaginable heights.

At this point it is worth observing that even for the scientist, evolution is a probability statement, rather than a statement of absolute or eternal truth. After all, evolution if it be so, has worked so slowly over such long periods, hundreds of thousands of years of geological time, that no one has observed it as such or therefore been able to verify it infallibly.

However, what we can say is that some form of development in the natural order would very clearly seem to have happened. How should the Christian respond?

CHRISTIAN RESPONSE

First of all the Christian, taking his Bible seriously, would have to oppose the anti-Christian version of evolutionary theory which removes God entirely from the process. This form of evolutionary theory has been used to propagate atheism, communism and much anti-God thought and behaviour.

Apart from that, it explains nothing. It doesn't say, as we observed earlier, what set the stage for the process, what started it, or what keeps it going. While it speaks dogmatically of evolution as scientific law it fails to recognise that even established scientific law is not the cause of a series of events but only a generalised description of events which seem to be related. The law of gravity doesn't make a pear fall to the ground. It just describes some force which does!

One religious accommodation of the theory is called *Theistic Evolution*. This view puts God into the evolutionary process and makes creation, as it were, happen from within the process. God and created reality are in some way integrated and matter is almost accorded a divine psychic energy or consciousness. Nature and Supernature, God and His creation are integrally wedded, almost dissolved into one to the point where the natural almost swallows up the supernatural.

By this view there is an unbroken line from the original cells on the prehistoric waters to man. Man becomes a sudden, even supernatural, mutation within the process.

Many Christians have accepted this view.

However, beyond this view is yet another and probably more Biblical view mentioned earlier called *Progressive Creation*. This says that God is not trapped or locked into the process but is above it, apart from it, transcendent over it and yet directing it. There is thus no unbroken line from the amoeba to man. Rather, the great species and families of creatures came about not by some magical unexplained process, nor by some divine power within evolution, but by the constant creative and everactive power of a transcendent God.

In this view we don't dogmatise about time in creation nor are we obliged to understand the Genesis 'day' (Hebrew *Yom*) as referring to a twenty-four-hour period but conceivably to an era or span of time, as we might speak of 'Julius Caesar's day' – i.e. the period when Julius Caesar lived.

Professor Bernard Ramm, however, concludes in his superb volume *The Christian View of Science and Scripture*, that making *Yom* refer to an epoch is

problematic from a linguistic point of view and he prefers
to see the six days as the period over which creation was
revealed rather than performed. The six days then become
six picture days or six days of revelation.

The process of revelation would thus be – Light (Day
One), Firmament (Day Two), Earth, Sea and Vegetation
(Day Three), Sun, Moon, Stars (Day Four), Birds and
Fishes (Day Five), Animals, Reptiles and Man (Day Six).

Ramm partly inclines to this view because of the
scientific difficulty of fitting the geological and biological
data into six epochs in *The Biblical Order* as outlined
above. The most obvious difficulty is the creation of
astronomical bodies on the fourth day – i.e. after the
earth![24]

On the other hand, if that picture of the sun, moon and
stars was revealed to the writer on the fourth day – or else if
that is the order in which it would appear to a man had he
been there to observe – then we can make some sense of the
Biblical order.

One would also add that the view of Progressive
Creation allows for God not only speaking the word
(called *fiat creation*) at key moments in the process, but
also implanting His Spirit in Nature so that the laws of
nature, directed by God's Spirit, bring about over
enormous periods of time, the plan of God. This
progressive creation thus becomes DIVINE CREATION
ACCORDING TO LAW.

In this view the relative lateness of Biblical man and the
great antiquity of fossil man (say, 500,000 years) may be
handled by a recognition of the possibility of some sort of
sub-human, pre-human, or pre-Adamic creature which
stood on two legs and was physiologically similar to man.

Commenting on the creation story, John Stott writes:

Not many Christians today imagine that the 'days' of creation
were intended to be understood as precise periods of twenty-
four hours each. Indeed, speaking for myself, I cannot see that
at least some forms of the theory of evolution contradict or are

contradicted by the Genesis revelation. Scripture reveals religious truths about God, that He created all things by His word, that His creation was 'good', and that His creative programme culminated in man; science suggests that 'evolution' may have been the mode which God employed in creating.

To suggest this tentatively need not in any way detract from man's uniqueness. I myself believe in the historicity of Adam and Eve as the original couple from whom the human race is descended. But my acceptance of Adam and Eve as historical is not imcompatible with my belief that several forms of pre-Adamic hominid may have existed for thousands of years previously. These hominids began to advance culturally. They made their cave drawings and buried their dead. It is conceivable that God created Adam out of one of them. You may call them *homo erectus*, I think you may even call some of them *homo sapiens*, for these are arbitrary scientific names. But Adam was the first *homo divinus*, if I may coin the phrase, the first man to whom may be given the Biblical designation 'made in the image of God'. Precisely what the divine likeness was, which was stamped upon him, we do not know, for Scripture nowhere tells us. But Scripture seems to suggest that it included rational, moral, social and spiritual faculties which make man unlike all other creatures and like God the creator, and on account of which he was given 'dominion' over the lower creation.[25]

THE POINT

The point in all of this is to see that Genesis is primarily a religious statement. 'How? What? and When?' are the scientists' questions, but the Bible's questions are 'Who? Whence? Whither? and Why?' These are the religious questions.

Science describes processes and seeks to relate apparently unrelated facts. But it does not provide ultimate explanations. Genesis however purports to explain man's existence, not in terms of biological or physical facts, but in terms of meaning, purpose and divine accountability.

What we cannot allow as Christians is the view that the universe and nature are self-creating. Besides, a godless evolution has to contend with the law of *entropy* which speaks of loss of energy in the universe and affirms that every ordered arrangement tends to become disordered. Entropy is a random, disorderly process by which things degenerate. Life is an ordered process by which things build and progress in order and are generated. From where, in the view of godless, mechanical evolution, does this integrating, life-giving energy come from to keep conquering the more basic laws and disintegrating processes of entropy?

The Christian answer is that this energy and power come from God. And although there are still problems and mysteries with this view, it nevertheless places less strain on our credulity and on our intellectual processes, than the view which says we and everything around us arrived through some mind-boggling combination of impersonal energy flirting over limitless periods of time with the mysterious maiden of chance.

What we can say more positively is that the theory of evolution is at this point in time considered the best description of the development of living things which science can give, though like all theories of science, it is open to modification as new evidence comes to light. But at best it is only a description of a process.

Genesis says that whatever the process, the author of all is God. And whether He acted by a series of mighty instantaneous acts or by a process is not consequential. It would be equally divine either way.

So we come back to where we started to affirm with Genesis that 'In the beginning God...' That's the key thing to say.

There is only one thing more key to say. And now it is the beginning of the New Testament, and not the beginning of the Old, which says it. And it is this.

'In the beginning was the Word and the Word was with God and the Word was God. All things were made through Him and without Him was not anything made that was made . . . AND-THE-WORD-BECAME-FLESH-AND-DWELT-AMONG-US . . .' (John 1:1–3).

The Word became flesh? He who made everything became flesh? He who is behind the whole creative process became a human?

That's right. On the first Christmas Day. That's what I'm saying. That's the Biblical claim.

Let's look at it.

Chapter Nine

CHRISTMAS HISTORY

Christianity had come to seem to us probable. It all
hinged on Jesus. Was He, in fact, the Lord Messiah, the
Holy One of Israel, the Christ? Was He, indeed, the
Incarnate God? Very God of very God? This was the
heart of the matter.

Sheldon Vanauken

Today is Christmas Day. From my window at Kenton-on-
Sea, beautiful, gentle Kenton, in South Africa's Eastern
Cape, I look out on the expansive, shimmering mouth of
the Bushman's River pressing itself into the Indian Ocean,
knowing that in an hour or so, the tide will turn and the
Indian Ocean will press Bushman's back with even more
resolution. And the fish will come. And fishermen luckier
than I will catch them. Fish – symbols here of angling skill
and sport. And fun. And quietness. Alone. But long ago,
symbols of Christ. And still today.

The acrostic said IXTHEUS – Greek for a fish. *Iesus
Xristos Theou Uios Soter* – meaning Jesus Christ Son of
God and Saviour. For muddled, panting, persecuted
Christians the picture of the fish scratched on prison cell
or catacomb said it all. Jesus Christ was, and is, son of God
and Saviour.

And that's what our children and their cousins
celebrated last night when they put on their own nativity
play for all of us oldies – mums and dads, grandparents,

uncles and aunts. There was the stage set for us with
manger, crib and straw, the latter in the form of cardboard
stuffing which later took for ever and a day to clean up.
And a lantern burning with a real flame to light the make-
shift stable in grandpa's lounge. And a star glittering in
tinsel from a window ledge. And to crown it an almost
Shakespearean banner, well worthy of Stratford-upon-
Avon, and all bedecked in Christmas colours and motif
pasted to the wall, and announcing boldly: *'Welcome!
Christmas punch and pudding will be served afterwards –
Merry Christmas.'*

And, of course, there were the players. Gareth and
Bridgie were Joseph and Mary respectively – the
seriousness of childlike faith etched in every shy expression of face or movement. Debbie, Jackie and baby
Lulu were radiant junior angels, with haloed Cathy very
much the angel in charge of proceedings, not only with
her 'one, two, three' before each carol, but with her
promptings of any almost fallen angel who looked like
forgetting heaven's script. My Marty, moustachioed for the
occasion, looked more like a Mexican gangster than one of
the Magi, while his cousin, the other Marty, perpetually
wore that look of quizzical doubt which spoke volumes of
hesitation about shepherding as any long-term thing for
him. Finally there was mischievous Richard – as a most
serious and pensive little donkey with floppy ears who
moved back and forth across centre-stage, seemingly in
two minds as to whether to bolt for it or stay to represent a
gazing and adoring creation.

Then came with well-rehearsed and flawless precision,
the familiar Christmas story. First the Bible text:

'About this time Caesar Augustus, the Roman Emperor,
decreed that a census should be taken throughout the nation.
(This census was taken when Quirinius was governor of
Syria.) Everyone was required to return to his ancestral home
for this registration. And because Joseph was a member of the
royal line, he had to go to Bethlehem in Judea, King David's

ancient home - journeying there from the Galilean village of Nazareth. He took with him Mary, his fiancée, who was obviously pregnant by this time. And while they were there, the time came for her baby to be born; and she gave birth to her first child, a son' (Luke 2:1-6).

Then the bits about the shepherds, the wise men, Herod and so on. And finally carols. Immortal carols: 'Hark, the Herald Angels Sing', 'Silent Night', 'The First Noel'. And the little town of Bethlehem:

> How still we see thee lie,
> Above thy deep and dreamless sleep,
> The silent stars go by,
> Yet in thy dark street shineth
> The everlasting light,
> The hopes and fears of all the years
> Are met in thee tonight.

And time stood still while children told the Christmas story, as only children can tell it. Oh, it was magic! The stuff memories are made of. And the fairy tale atmosphere of beauty, wonder and goodness. And faith. Childlike faith. Perhaps children should be the only people allowed to preach at Christmas because they really believe it. All of which gets us to the big question - Is it fact? Or fairy tale? Is this that same God of Genesis now stepping in human form on to Planet Earth?

THE CHRIST OF HISTORY

Actually what we have to decide is whether the Christmas pageantry and ritual which we all go through annually is really just a beautiful fairy tale which children believe, as they believe in Santa Claus, or whether in very truth we are speaking here of the central, pivotal, foundational fact of all history. When children perform a nativity play most adults watch it with that same charmed indulgence they

reserve for other childish whims about fairies or reindeers
on the roof on Christmas Eve. It is sweet, even moving, but
in the words of one of Gershwin's songs in *Porgy and Bess*,
'It ain't necessarily so'. In fact most would be more
emphatic: 'It just isn't true. It's a beautiful story but it has
no substance in factual history.'

But that is just where we could be most dreadfully
wrong. In fact the X-factor in Xmas is so compelling and
mysterious that it deserves consideration from several
angles. For it is either very much more than a Christmas
fairy tale or else very much less. It is either the supreme
event of all history or the planet's most perilous hoax. It is
either the plainest clue man has to the meaning of things
or the most dangerous bit of self-deception ever foisted on
the human race. The Incarnation of Jesus is either the
universe entering a new phase of its life or it is just another
human birth, little different from that of any other great
man. There are no halfway houses.

Christians are saying that the God we have talked about,
and for whose existence we have hopefully seen considerable evidence in the four preceding chapters, actually
became man in that first Christmas. Nothing more.
Nothing less. And they believe that it is this Incarnation
which illumines and integrates the whole mass of our
knowledge and experience. And they believe in it, as they
believe in the sun, not only because they see it but because
by it they see everything else.

However, none of this will become real for anyone until
or unless they can believe that we are here dealing with
historical fact and not childish phantasy. After all,
Christianity is, according to its own claim, primarily a
self-revelation of God in a historical person and in that
person's life, death and resurrection. It is therefore open to
criticism and attack on historical grounds as no other
religion is.

INCREDIBLE OR PROBABLE

Of course the very thought that God Himself could actually step on to our planet in real time and space and history would seem at one level incredible. Yet if we can accept that there is someone personal (we'll call Him X) behind reality as we know it, then it is not illogical or indeed improbable to suppose that such a personality would reveal itself to other persons in His universe. And if those persons happen to be on Planet Earth this will involve a personal and historical intrusion on Planet Earth.

Now if X as personal is anything like man as personal (which the Bible says He is) then we can also say one very vital thing about X. Simply on the basis of what we know from ourselves about the nature of personality, we can affirm that X will want to reveal Himself to other persons.

Look at it this way. Suppose you and one other person were cast up on a desert island after a shipwreck. You could no more sit 30 yards away from the other person and not communicate than fly to the moon. It would be a plain, straightforward expression of the nature of personality to communicate. Every last instinct of personhood would be denied if the two of you sat 30 yards apart like a couple of logs, without talking or revealing yourselves to each other.

It is likewise inconceivable that the personal X behind all the universe and the one responsible for us as personal beings should stand back at His end of the universe, as it were, and never reveal Himself to us at the other end! A self-revelation of X in human history not only stands as a possibility (seeing He has all power) but as a thorough-going probability (seeing He is personal). If God is personal, His self-revelation is probable.

Beyond that we would have to say that an effective revelation of that Ultimate Personality requires the Perfect Person – One who will show in an earthly life what God is always.

The question then comes. Is there anywhere in our planet's life and history where there is a claim of any sort that X is indeed revealing Himself in the perfect person? The answer of course is obvious. There is only one such claim and there is only one such person, Jesus of Nazareth, born as the Christmas Babe of Bethlehem. He is indeed the X factor in Xmas!

UNUSUAL INTERRUPTION

Of course the problem for our poor old minds is that history seems to us to be so uniform, predictable, invariable and steady that we can't really conceive of such an unusual interruption as the one we are talking about.

However, if there is in fact a personal mind and will behind everything, then it should not be too mind-boggling to see both the uniform course of life and the unusual variable as equally grounded in that same mind and will with both the uniformity and the variability each revealing something different about X.

For example, if I am home every night from work at 5 p.m. 364 days of the year, but I decide on the 365th evening to return at 9 p.m. both the regular schedule and the exceptional departure from it are grounded in my own mind and will and purpose. I am free and able to make the exception happen if my mind decrees it for some reason and my will decides it should be so. Moreover the uniformity would reveal that I am disciplined, regular, predictable, reliable, orderly, devoted to my family and capable of planning. On the other hand, the unusual deviation and exception, say because I came across an accident on the highway, would say not only that I am compassionate and caring but that my nature judges a deed of mercy and compassion in a special moment of need as more important than my accustomed regularity at that point. Thus the unusual variation (i.e. the abnormal interruption of the regular), would say something which the regularity concealed – namely my commitment to the absolute primacy of mercy and compassion. But what controls both my regularity and my interruption of it is the same principle – namely my mind, will and purpose as an expression of who I am.

Thus from what we already know from life about how we reveal our own natures to others, there is nothing inconceivable, or out of character in the notion that the *mind*, *will* and *purpose* of God may decree not only the regularity of the universe, which says certain things about God's nature, but the occasional interruption of it (a miracle from our point of view) which reveals other things. The interruption, which in this discussion is God's historical incarnation in Jesus, was an act of self-revelation and caring appropriate to the needs of the human race at that moment and in line with the character and purposes of God. Why should we cast that out as so impossible?

Once God had chosen at creation to be related to man, He accepted responsibility for something outside of Himself and an act of self-revelation on His part became inevitable. Moreover, if this personal God is good and therefore eager to bless and help a lost and confused human race, it should not be surprising to us that He should want to convey to us what our problems are and how to solve them. And there was no way to do this other than through some happening in history.

That happening took place at that first Christmas long ago. It was not the birth of a fairy tale. It was the universe changing gear as God interrupted the ordinary, regular course of things to do something unique for us and tell us something quite new about Himself and His love for us.

Chapter Ten

TRUSTING THE TEXT

One of the many divine qualities of the Bible is this, that it does not yield its secrets to the irreverent and censorious.

James Packer

Given our affirmation in the last chapter that the Christmas story is indeed historical, it is probable that someone will be asking whether the Bible, which gives us this story, is not itself unreliable and unhistorical – a sort of hotch-potch of views and expressions of faith penned by well-meaning but gullible disciples scores or hundreds of years after Christ and projecting back on to Him some hopes and dreams and wishful thinking.

It is important to establish rightaway that we aren't asking enquirers to accept the Bible blindly. Far from it. The Christian invites the application of the appropriate tests of authenticity which are applied to any supposedly historical documents and he invites the enquirer to give the documents the benefit of the doubt, as he would with any ancient historical document, until such time as the text disqualifies itself by known factual inaccuracy or hopeless internal inconsistencies.

WEALTH OF MANUSCRIPTS

One test which is often applied to ancient books is the so-called Bibliographical Test.

This relates to the number, value, condition and age of the documents themselves and the process by which they came to us. This is all important for the New Testament as we cannot possess the actual documents as penned by Matthew, Mark, Luke, John or Paul.

In all this the New Testament scores very well and comes out better than any of the ancient writings of antiquity.

For example the huge number of New Testament manuscripts or portions thereof (some 13,000 in all) means that the text as originally penned can be established beyond reasonable doubt.

Of the variant readings only about one-sixtieth rise above the trivial into the substantial and this would mathematically work out at a text that is 98.33 per cent pure.[26]

The way this is worked out is in its simplest terms something like this. You start with the original text. This is then copied. From the first copies others are made, And so on. Look at it like a sort of family tree.

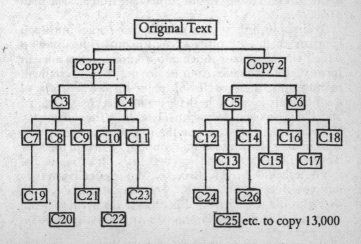

Now supposing copies 1 to 18 are lost. Yet, if you have copies 19 to 13,000 you can see, by comparing copy with copy, how easy it becomes, seeing no two copyists are likely to make the same mistakes, to spot deviations, errors, double copying or whatever till finally you get back to the *original text*.

Beyond that it is worth realising that we cannot be sceptical about New Testament history without becoming sceptical of knowing anything at all about ancient history. If one accepts in broad substance what was written by Caesar, Livy, Tacitus, Plato or Herodotus, one must on the same grounds accept the writings of Matthew, Mark, Luke, John and Paul. In the first place the number of available New Testament manuscripts is overwhelmingly greater than those of any other work of ancient literature. Secondly, the manuscripts which we have of the New Testament were written closer to the date of the original writing than is true of almost any other items of ancient literature. The earliest fragment, the so-called John Ryland manuscript housed in the John Ryland library of Manchester, is a portion of St John's Gospel and is dated about AD130. The rest of our copies date from AD200 up to AD500.

At first blush these all seem very late copies until you compare them with other ancient manuscript copies on which we in fact base much of our knowledge of ancient history. In dramatic contrast to the New Testament manuscripts, these copies of major historical works of authority are found to be between 800 years (e.g. Tacitus) and 1300 years (e.g. Herodatus) later than their originals. But we nevertheless accept their general accuracy and genuineness. How much more should we accept the New Testament? If you want to check this out, look at the footnote below by F.F. Bruce of Manchester University and you'll see what I mean.* You may also like to look over the useful chart on this, drawn up by my friend, Norman Allchin of Australia (see Appendix, page 183).

---

*Perhaps we can appreciate how wealthy the New Testament is in

F J H Hort of Cambridge University, who spent twenty-eight years studying the New Testament text (an achievement, said a fellow scholar, 'never surpassed in the scholarship of any country'), concluded: 'In the variety and fullness of the evidence on which it rests the text of the New Testament stands absolutely and unapproachably alone among ancient writings.'[28]

TEXT ITSELF

When we look at the New Testament itself, we quickly feel what Bible translator J. B. Phillips called 'the ring of truth'. We also sense a deep commitment to historical accuracy. Just listen to Peter when he affirms: 'We have not been telling you fairy tales when we explained to you the power of our Lord Jesus Christ and His coming again. My own eyes have seen His splendour and His glory' (2 Pet. 1:16).

John is likewise equally emphatic when he reiterates that he is bringing eye-witness testimony: 'Again I say, we

---

manuscript attestation if we compare the textual material for other ancient historical works. For Caesar's Gallic Wars (composed between 58 and 50 BC) there are several extant MSS, but only nine or ten are good, and the oldest is some 900 years later than Caesar's day. Of the 142 books of the Roman History of Livy (59 BC–AD 17), only 35 survive; these are known to us from not more than 20 MSS of any consequence, only one of which, and that containing fragments of Books III–VI, is as old as the fourth century. Of the 14 books of the Histories of Tacitus (c.AD 100) only four and a half survive; of the 16 books of his Annals, 10 survive in full and two in part. The text of these extant portions of his two great historical works depends entirely on two MSS, one of the ninth century and one of the eleventh. The extant MSS of his minor works (Dialogus de Oratoribus, Agricola, Germania) all descend from a codex of the tenth century. The History of Thucydides (c.460–400 BC) is known to us from eight MSS, the earliest belonging to c.AD 900, and a few papyrus scraps, belonging to about the beginning of the Christian era. The same is true of the History of Herodotus (488–428BC). Yet no classical scholar would listen to an argument that the authenticity of Herodotus or Thucydides is in doubt because the earliest MSS of their works which are of any use to us are over 1,300 years later than the originals.[27]

are telling you about what we ourselves have actually seen and heard, so that you may share the fellowship and the joys we have with the Father and with Jesus Christ His son' (1 John 1:3).

This eye-witness appeal is very striking. These men were talking about things they had seen and heard and in the case of Luke about things he had carefully researched from others who had seen and heard (e.g. Luke 1:1–3). Later of course, as a travelling companion with Paul, he was personally in on many of the adventures described in the Book of Acts (e.g. Acts 16:10, 12, 16).

Clearly these early writers also had to contend with many people, some quite hostile, who were acquainted with the basic facts relating to the life and work of Jesus. So they could not afford to risk inaccuracies (not to speak of deliberate manipulation of the facts), which would at once be exposed by those who would be only too glad to embarrass them by exposing their distortions or false statements.

And lest we imagine that these writings were faked or were penned by men whose memories had all failed them, it is worth noting that the interval between the events described and the moment they were catalogued in the Biblical text is not substantial. The earliest documents can probably be dated about eighteen or twenty years after the death of Jesus. That would be like writing in 1985 about the Israeli-Egypt Six Day War in 1967. Then the latest New Testament documents are probably no later than AD 90 which puts them sixty years after Jesus' earthly life.* That would be like an old man in 1985 writing about life in the years after the First World War. I know an old man who fought in the trenches in the First World War and he

---

*Nelson Glueck, at one time probably the foremost Biblical archaeologist in the world, said 'We can say emphatically that there is no longer any solid basis for dating any book of the New Testament after about AD 80.'[29] Not all scholars would agree exactly with that, but very few would date these later New Testament documents beyond AD 90.

can describe all the details of that horrific experience better than he can tell you about what he did last week!

This is not to suggest that there are no internal problems with the New Testament text. But Biblical scholarship is there to grapple with these and seek further light. In fact numerous so-called difficulties with the text have been resolved even during this century and we have no reason to suppose that this process will not continue as dedicated, godly and reverent scholars, as against destructive sceptics, work with the data at hand.

NON BIBLICAL SOURCES

It is also worth noting that there are other sources, external to the text itself. Do these confirm and substantiate the New Testament facts or contradict and refute them?

Clearly this is a huge field and one cannot explore it fully here. However, one can affirm that evidence from other ancient documents, some by secular writers, makes clear that the historical nature of Jesus as a person is not open to dispute. He is axiomatic for all historians and no serious scholar, probably not even in the Soviet Union, would venture now to postulate the non-historicity of Jesus.

Thus the Roman historian Tacitus (AD 55–120) in his *Annals* (Book XV.44) can speak of Jesus' death by crucifixion under Pontius Pilate during the reign of Tiberius, while Suetonius (AD 69–141), another Roman historian at the court of Hadrian, refers to the disturbances the Christians were making 'at the instigation of Chrestus', another spelling for Christ. (*Life of Claudius* 25:4.)

Then there is the famous lament from Pliny the Younger, a governor of Bithynia in Asia Minor. Writing in AD 112 to the Emperor Trajan he asks counsel on how to handle these tiresome Christians who meet regularly 'on a certain fixed day' to sing a hymn 'to Christ as God' (*Epistles X:96*).

Then there is Lucian, a second-century satirist, who spoke scornfully of Christ as 'the man who was crucified in Palestine because he introduced this new cult into the world'.

Other fascinating historical allusions are found in the writings of Josephus, the second-century Jewish historian (see *Antiquities* XVIII:33) and Tertullian (AD 155-200), a jurist-theologian in Carthage who found himself pleading the Christian case before the Roman authorities of North Africa.

Other confirming external evidence comes from the breathtaking range of archaeological discovery and research.

Archaeological data has confirmed not only the Christmas story in its broad outlines but thousands of other Biblical references. In fact St Luke comes out of archaeological studies particularly well. Sir William Ramsay, one of our age's greatest archaeologists wrote 'Luke is a historian of the first rank: not merely are his statements of fact trustworthy; he is possessed of the true historic sense. This author should be placed along with the very greatest historians.'[30]

Prof. E M Blaiklock, who was professor of classics at Auckland University, adds his conclusions on Luke, saying 'Luke is a consummate historian, to be ranked in his own right with the great writers of the Greeks.'[31] Nelson Glueck wrote: 'It may be stated categorically that no archaeological discovery has ever controverted a Biblical reference.'[32]

Prof. Millar Burrows, the Yale University archaeologist, puts it succinctly: 'On the whole, archaeological work has unquestionably strengthened confidence in the reliability of the Scriptural record.'[33] And when the available data is not accepted by some scholars, he sees it as stemming not from careful evaluation 'but from an enormous pre-disposition against the supernatural'.[34]

CONCLUSION

So then, the New Testament text emerges as a document you can trust. This means that when you next see some little children doing a nativity play – or when you next sing or hear a Christmas carol – you don't have to feel an indulgent and tolerant scepticism, as of a beautiful fairy tale, but rather you can sit on the edge of your chair as a convinced historian who has been overwhelmed with the truth of something factual.

Chapter Eleven

THE INCOMPARABLE CHRIST

I believe there is no one lovelier, deeper, more
sympathetic and more perfect than Jesus. I say to myself
that not only is there no one else like Him, but there
never could be any one like Him.

Feodor Dostoevski

That a person called Jesus was born in Palestine round
about the beginning of this era is, as we have said, beyond
historical dispute. That He lived and died is unquestion-
able. That He was a remarkable person no one will
contest. But whether He was in some way God in the flesh
is where the argument begins. Here is where the mind
boggles and where faith fumbles. So we must press
forward in the next few chapters and look first at His
remarkable claims, then at the astounding view of Him
which the Apostles reached and which they have given us
in the Scriptures, and finally we must reflect on the
massively exciting claim that He rose from the dead and is
alive today.

EXTRAORDINARY PERSON

At the very, very least both the New Testament text and
subsequent history of the world show an extraordinary
human being. This is well summarised in the anonymous,

celebrated poetic statement on Jesus called *One Solitary Life.*

He was born in an obscure village, the child of a peasant woman. He grew up in still another village, where He worked in a carpenter's shop until He was 30. Then for three years He was an itinerant preacher. He never wrote a book. He never held an office. He never had a family or owned a house. He didn't go to college. He never visited a big city. He never travelled 200 miles from the place where He was born. He did none of the things one usually associates with greatness. He had no credentials but Himself. He was only 33 when the tide of public opinion turned against Him. His friends ran away. He was turned over to His enemies and went through the mockery of a trial. He was nailed to a cross between two thieves. While He was dying, His executioners gambled for His clothing, the only property He had on earth. When He was dead, He was laid in a borrowed grave through the pity of a friend. Nineteen centuries have come and gone and today He is the central figure of the human race and the leader of mankind's progress. All the armies that ever marched, all the navies that ever sailed, all the parliaments that ever sat, all the kings that ever reigned, put together, have not affected the life of man on this earth as much as that ONE SOLITARY LIFE.

It is true. No other influence has so mightily touched our planet as that brought by the simple life of Jesus of Nazareth.

So we should not be surprised if the New Testament picture of Him is indeed the right one. The hard fact is that the New Testament presents Him as God in the flesh, God the Creator, stepping right onto our planet. Mind blowing. But there it is!

GOD IN THE FLESH

I remember once some years ago chatting to a student in one of South Africa's leading universities.

'Oh! I think this whole Christianity thing is so boring and tedious,' he said.

'Now listen to this,' I replied. 'You've heard the words before – but just listen to them again. They come from the opening chapter of John's Gospel. "In the beginning was the Word, and the Word was with God – AND THE WORD WAS GOD ... AND THE WORD BECAME FLESH AND DWELT AMONG US."

'Now get this,' I went on to my student friend, 'don't let the familiarity of the words blunt or dull their force to your heart and mind – THE WORD WAS GOD – got it? GOD. The Word was GOD – AND THE WORD *BECAME FLESH* and dwelt among us.

'It's breathtaking,' I said. 'Quite breathtaking. The Word was God and *the Word became flesh, became a human and actually dwelt among other humans on this earth.* They saw Him, experienced Him, touched Him, talked to Him and then put down their experiences of Him on paper so we could get the picture too.'

'When you put it that way I can see it is pretty amazing,' said the student.

UNIFYING POWER

Let's look more closely at what St John is saying in his Gospel. You may remember my mentioning that when the Greeks looked out at the universe they saw it as a reality which cohered together in a unity. (NB: Unus = Latin for one; versus = Latin for turned. The reality around us was 'unus-versus'. A universe – i.e. turned into one.) Somewhere, somehow there was an inner unifying principle. What that was they didn't know, but they called it the 'Logos'. The Greek noun literally means 'a word' or 'a self-expression'. It referred to that dynamic and mighty controlling, unifying and creating power which lay at the heart of creation.

Now along comes St John. What he says to the Greeks is

this. 'You're right. Your so-called Logos is behind everything, creating it, uniting it, keeping it all going. Indeed that Logos was there in the beginning, it was with God and in fact it was God. Not only that, but the Logos was the agent through which "all things were made" (v.3). In a nutshell "the world was made through Him" (v.10), as you Greeks have already concluded.'

With all of that the average Greek would have been at peace. Then comes John's uppercut. His sensational thunderbolt.

'Come now, you Greeks, get this. This Logos which was the creating, unifying force behind the universe, this Logos which was God Himself, yes, this same Logos "became-flesh-and-dwelt-among-us"' (v.14).

John goes on. 'What's more, the enfleshed Logos manifested a character which was "FULL of Grace and Truth"'. How did John know? Because 'we beheld His Glory'. In other words, 'We saw it all with our own eyes. We are eye-witnesses.'

Later John opens one of his letters underlining the first-hand nature of his testimony: 'Christ was alive when the world began, yet I myself have seen Him with my own eyes and listened to Him speak. I have touched Him with my own hands. He is God's message of Life. This one who is life from God has been shown to us and we guarantee that we have seen Him.'[35]

This same thought is eloquently taken up by St Paul:

Christ is the exact likeness of the unseen God. He existed before God made anything at all, and, in fact, Christ Himself is the creator who made everything in heaven and earth, the things we can see and the things we cannot; the spirit world with its kings and kingdoms, its rulers and authorities; all were made by Christ for His own use and glory. He was before all else began and it is His power that holds everything together.[36]

NO PARALLEL

Now these are astonishing statements and right off they alert us to the fact that we cannot set Jesus into any general pantheon of gods or into any line up of leaders of other religions. You can't put Jesus, Mohammed, Confucius and Buddha in the same category. Jesus doesn't fit. His claims were of a different order.

C S Lewis commented on this point in these terms:

> There is no half-way house, and there is no parallel in other religions. If you had gone to Buddha and asked him: 'Are you the son of Bramah?' he would have said, 'My son, you are still in the veil of illusion.' If you had gone to Socrates and asked, 'Are you Zeus?' he would have laughed at you. If you had gone to Mohammed and asked, 'Are you Allah?' he would first have rent his clothes and then cut off your head. If you had asked Confucius, 'Are you heaven?' I think he would probably have replied, 'Remarks which are not in accordance with nature are in bad taste.'[37]

JESUS' CLAIMS

But as we reflect on Jesus' claims we quickly see several things. First of all we shall see that the supernatural Christ of faith is also the Jesus of the early evangelists. The supernatural Christ is not a later literary creation. In fact there is no record in existence – if we are concerned with history from the Gospel sources – which knows anything of a non-supernatural Jesus, except by tampering with the text under the pressure of naturalistic presuppositions.

Secondly, we shall see that these claims were light-years away from anything any other sane religious leaders have ever said. This is obviously not to say that there is no truth in other religions. Obviously from nature, the world around us, and our own inner beings, a tremendous body of spiritual truth can be gleaned. And the great religious geniuses of history who founded the other great religions have had access to this data which Christians call General Revelation. At this level Christians do not have a monopoly on God and His truth. They share large bodies of common truth with other religions. But Christians believe that everything in other religions which is authentically true finds fulfilment, climax and completion in Christ as the universal and as the ultimate revelation.

In other words the question as to whether all religions are equally valid and whether all are paths on the way to the same goal answers itself for each person as they answer the old question 'What think ye of Christ? Whose Son is He?' (Matt. 22:42).

All of this becomes very obvious once we look at the claims themselves. Some of these are very direct, some are less direct and some relate to titles which Jesus took upon Himself.

EGOCENTRIC

Take for example Jesus' exclusive claim in John 14:6. These words simply take the breath away. Jesus said, 'I am the Way, the Truth and the Life. No one comes to the Father but by me' (John 14:6). This is a staggering example of the egocentricity of so many of Jesus' claims. Where other religious leaders point away to God and say, 'That is the Way, that is the Truth, that is the Life', Jesus says, 'I am the Way, I am the Truth, I am the Life.' Indeed He goes further and says, 'No one comes to the Father but by me.'

This sort of thing was as bewildering to the ears of the disciples and to others who heard Him as it is when it first comes to us. No wonder people said, 'Never did a man speak like this man' (John 7:46). Indeed never before had anyone come along and spoken in such egocentric terms and yet urged humility on other people.

So it is that Jesus can also say 'I am the bread of life . . . I am the water of life . . . I am the good shepherd . . . I am the resurrection and the life . . . He who believes in me though he die, yet shall he live; and whoever lives and believes in me shall never die.' This is amazing.

Even more amazing is the fact that at the end of the day we do not have the impression of a proud person. Imagine asking Shakespeare, Milton and Goethe to lock themselves away for six months and bring their combined genius to bear upon the task of creating a character who speaks all the time about himself and yet finally gives the impression of overwhelming humility. I am sure they would throw in the sponge at the beginning of the assignment.

JEWISH CONTEXT

We also note that Jesus, who was living and teaching in a monotheistic Jewish society, where religious faith was appropriately to be placed only in Jehovah God, could actually urge people to believe and place religious faith in Him. In fact, He could not only say 'believe in God, believe also in me' (John 14:1) but He could actually say that eternal life was reserved for those who placed their total faith in Him and gave their full religious allegiance to Him. Said He, 'Whoever lives and believes in ME shall never die' (John 11:26). The sheer audacity of this sort of statement quite boggles the mind.

Beyond that we actually find Him claiming identity with Jehovah God. When the bewildered and confused disciple, Philip, said to Him 'Lord show us the Father and we will be satisfied' (John 14:8), Jesus retorts with the staggering question 'Have I been with you so long and yet you do not know me, Philip? He who has seen me has seen the Father; how can you say "Show us the Father"?' (John 14:9).

As if that wasn't startling enough, He then went on to say that He would be the one who would raise people up at the final day of judgment. Thus in John 6:40, He can say, 'This is the will of my Father that every one who sees the son and believes in Him should have eternal life'. Then He adds of the person who does so believe in Him, 'I will raise him up at the last day.'

It was presumably this sort of self-understanding which allowed Him to receive the worship normally reserved in that culture for God alone. Although the Old Testament commandment said 'Thou shalt worship the Lord thy God and Him only shalt thou serve', Jesus could come along and allow the leper in Matthew 8:2 to 'adore Him' (i.e. worship Him). Then there was a man born blind who after being healed 'fell down and worshipped Him' (John 9:35–9). Matthew also tells us that the disciples 'adored Him', saying, 'Truly you are the Son of God' (Matt. 14:33).

MOST STARTLING

Most startling of all, perhaps, is the situation following the resurrection when He faces doubting Thomas. 'Put your finger here,' He says, 'and see my hands; and put out your hand and place it in my side; do not be faithless but believing' (John 20:27). Then Thomas responds and says to Him 'My Lord and my God'.

But instead of telling Thomas he has got the wrong end of the stick and that he can appropriately call Him master, rabbi or teacher, but not God, Jesus on the other hand accepts Thomas's worship, accepts Thomas's designation of Him as Lord and God and then responds to him, saying, 'Have you believed because you have seen me? Blessed are they who have not seen and yet believe' (John 20:27–9). Thomas is rebuked for his unbelief but not for his worship.

Jesus actually claims further that all power in the universe is His. Speaking to His disciples at the end of His earthly ministry, He told them to go out and proclaim His message to all the world and then added the comforting assurance for them, 'All power in heaven and on earth is committed to me. And lo, I am with you always, even to · the end of the world' (Matt. 28:18).

Having made that sort of claim it is not surprising then that He should also claim pre-existence. In an astonishing word to the religious leaders of the day, He said, 'Truly, truly I say to you, before Abraham was, I am.' We have to remember that 'I am' was the name or title by which God had revealed Himself to Moses. Here Jesus comes and prefaces His statement with a double amen (verily, verily) and thereby puts His statement in the form of the strongest oath possible and then uses of Himself the holy name of the divine being. The full implications of this are not lost upon the Jews who immediately seek to stone Him. Jesus here is using the formula for timelessness and the Jews knew that belonged to Jehovah God alone. For the local carpenter to take it upon Himself was to incur a religious crime worthy only of death. When one understands the Jewish view of Jehovah and the outrageous nature of the things Jesus was saying, it is not surprising that the Jews and especially their religious leaders were stirred to uncontrollable anger.

The climax of this came when He professed the right and authority to forgive sins. Having healed a paralysed man, He said to him, 'Your sins are forgiven you.' The horrified Jewish spectators respond, 'Why does this man speak that way? He is blaspheming; who can forgive sins but God alone?' (Mark 2:7). They all realised that while a person may forgive the injuries done to him by others, he certainly cannot forgive the sins done by another human being against God. Only God Himself can forgive that. Yet Jesus can say to the paralysed man who had in no way sinned against Him personally, 'Your sins are forgiven you.'

And so finally to His now inevitable arrest and trial.

ARREST AND TRIAL

The trial of Jesus was unique in the history of criminal trials in the sense that it was the identity not the actions of the accused which constituted the issue.

The question He was facing was this: 'Are you the Christ?' (Mark 14:61). Or 'Are you the Messiah of Jewish expectation?' Jesus' reply was, 'I am' (Mark 14:62).

In the other Gospels, Jesus' reported reply is, 'You have said so' (Matt. 26:64 – also Luke 23:3), which seems to be more evasive. But the Greek 'You say' (*humeis legete*) is just an idiom for 'yes'!

London lawyer Frank Morison noted:

> The formulae "Thou hast said', or 'Ye say that I am', which to modern ears sound evasive, had no such connotation to the contemporary Jewish mind. 'Thou sayest' was a traditional form in which a cultivated Jew replied to a question of grave or sad import. Courtesy forbade a direct 'yes' or 'no'.[38]

And if we are in any doubt as to the fact that Jesus answered affirmatively to the thousand-dollar question, we have only to see how the Jewish religious leaders responded. Representing the horror of the rest, the High Priest rent his garments and said 'He has uttered blasphemy. Why do we still need witnesses? You have now heard His blasphemy' (Matt. 26:65).

Not only had Jesus said 'Yes, I am the Christ', but He had also added, 'hereafter you will see the Son of man seated at the right hand of Power and coming on the clouds of heaven' (Matt. 26:64). Not only was 'Son of Man' a Messianic title, but 'the right hand of Power' was a phrase with powerful connotations of deity, while the idea of His 'coming on the clouds of heaven' spoke of that mighty moment at the end of the age when the Messiah Himself would consummate history.

Jesus thus stood self-condemned in the sight of the Jewish Sanhedrin who unanimously decreed His death.

He had made Himself out to be both Messiah and God. No wonder the High Priest rent his garment.*

Clearly we cannot view all these claims as anything other than totally extraordinary. To be sure, no other religious leader has ever made any comparable claims. But Jesus not only claimed deity, He has gone on to convince multitudes of this fact over the last twenty centuries. And those convinced include many of the finest intellectuals of history.

The fact is, as one writer noted, 'His teachings were ultimate, final – above those of Moses and the prophets. He never added any afterthoughts or revisions; He never retracted or changed; He never guessed, supposed, or spoke with any uncertainty. This is all so contrary to human teachers and teachings.'[40]

PERFECT LIFE

Now many people, as noted above, have made extravagant assertions about themselves, but their characters, either in the judgment of their contemporaries or of history or of both, have been unable to back up, support, substantiate or corroborate their claims.

Not so with Jesus. In His case His stupendous verbal claims were backed by a perfect life. That is the ultimate miracle. Those of us who seek to be bearers of the Christian message to others know the problems in a special way because we are endlessly aware of how

---

*Commenting on this, H B Swete, a great Greek scholar of the last century, noted: 'The law forbade the High Priest to rend his garment in private troubles (see Lev. 10:6 and 21:10), but when acting as a judge he was required by custom to express in this way his horror of any blasphemy uttered in his presence. The relief of the embarrassed judge is manifest. If trustworthy evidence was not forthcoming, the necessity for it had now been superseded; the Prisoner had incriminated Himself.'[39]

shamefully we fail to back the message we proclaim with the kind of quality lives which should go with it. Strive as we might, we know deeply that a chasm yawns between what we seek to teach of the Christian way and what we succeed in demonstrating in life.

But not so with Jesus. There was no gap at all between what He taught and what He was. Friends who knew Him intimately said He was 'a lamb without blemish or spot' (1 Pet. 1:19), one 'who did no sin' and in whose mouth was found 'no guile' (1 Pet. 2:22). John the Apostle, one of His very closest associates, affirmed, 'In Him is no sin' (1 John 3:5).

Even Jesus' enemies had to concede the point – 'This man was innocent', said the centurion (Luke 23:47). 'What evil has He done?' asked Pilate. 'I have sinned in betraying innocent blood', lamented remorseful Judas before taking his own life (Matt. 27:4).

NO SENSE OF GUILT

Even more startling is the fact that Jesus Himself seems void of that most elementary quality of moral life – a sense of guilt and failure. Indeed the greatest saints of history have of all people had the most acute sense of personal sinfulness. Isaiah had a vision of God and said 'Woe is me! For I am lost: for I am a man of unclean lips' (6:5). Suffering, saintly Job cried out, 'Now my eye sees thee; therefore I despise myself and repent in dust and ashes' (Job 42:5-6). David the Psalmist, the man after God's own heart, prayed, 'Wash me thoroughly from my iniquity and cleanse me from my sin' (Ps. 51:2). Peter, face to face with the power of Jesus, falls at His feet, saying, 'Depart from me, for I am a sinful man' (Luke 5:8). St Paul confessed, 'I am the foremost of sinners' (1 Tim. 1:15). In fact, the testimony of the ages is that to go on with God is to deepen in the awareness of personal shortcomings and sinfulness.

But for any such sense in Jesus, such as you would

expect in any great man of God, you will search in vain. In
fact, He went further. He did the unthinkable and actually
claimed sinlessness. 'Which of you convicts me of sin?' He
asked (John 8:46). 'I do always what is pleasing to him [my
Father]' (John 8:29). If anyone else spoke like that you
would despise him and disqualify him from being able to
teach you anything.

ULTIMATE CHARACTER

Someone said a bore is someone who keeps speaking about
himself when you want to talk about yourself! Like the
author at the drinks party who said: 'We've talked an
awful lot about me. Now let's talk about you. What do you
think of my new book?'

Such self-centred people bore us to tears and incur our
judgment. In the case of the mentally deranged they arouse
our pity.

Yet in the case of Jesus, instead of rejecting Him as
comical or pitiful or witty or worthy of only the most
modest attention, myriads in every age have fallen at His
feet in worship. They know that in Him they are seeing the
ultimate character – the character by which all others are
measured and who stands with a holiness, innocency,
spotless purity and love quite literally second to none. To
say someone is Christlike is to pay the ultimate tribute. On
the other hand, He Himself was compared to no one nor
ever has been, nor ever will be.

To absorb the staggering fact of Jesus' sinlessness
against the backdrop of our own self-recognised sinfulness
is to grasp that the supernatural in its most ultimate and
highest form is not in the miraculous demonstration of
power but in the moral demonstration of a perfect life. In
actual fact if we worked up a hypothesis of what God-
Incarnate would be like we should propose sinless
perfection and perfect sinlessness. And this is what we see

in Jesus. Our hypothesis and the observed facts of history coincide.

What then are the implications of all this? Well, there is a very basic one. We must decide whether Jesus really was who He said He was. I believe all our lives in time and all our destinies in eternity hang upon this verdict.

THE INVENTION OPTION

The options NOW before us are several. One is that the disciples invented the character of Jesus. This would make them the most brilliant of literary geniuses and at the same time the most despicable of rogues!

As to the brilliance, we know most of them were ordinary fishermen of modest intellect. They could not by any stretch of the imagination have invented the matchless character of Jesus. He is altogether too unpredictable and too extraordinary.

Beyond that this would be to make these simple writers greater than the hero. In fact the literary task is so out of the question that it would take a Christ to create a Christ. Moreover, the disciples could never have gone on to give the world the highest moral code it has ever known had the whole thing been one great concoction from the inner recesses of their rather average minds. Even less would they have been willing to die for it. You might die for an illusion, but not for a fraud.

THE DELUSION OPTION

So if the disciples recording the whole thing were not bad men busy deceiving the world, were they not perhaps just deluded themselves? Did they not face this Jesus and just make the wrong decision about Him?

Well. What were the options facing them? I believe they

had to decide, as do we, whether He was mad, bad, or God. They could see He wasn't just an ordinary bloke, let alone an ordinary prophet, because no ordinary prophet could take such breathtaking claims upon His lips if they were not true.

What in fact made those men and women accept His words was the perfect moral purity, strength and love with which they were faced when they met Jesus, not to mention the matchless height, depth and goodness of His teaching. They saw before them a character so unusual, so complete, so consistent, so perfect that the idea of His being a fraud, if at any time they entertained it, must have been quickly banished from their minds.

Clearly Jesus was not bad. Was He then mad? Was He someone suffering from hopeless megalomania and self-deception?

This idea just doesn't and can't fit the facts. Friend and foe alike agree that in Jesus we see an intellect and brain of penetrating brilliance, agility, lucidity and poetic genius. Most will agree He was the greatest teacher our world has ever known and the most morally incisive preacher ever to grace our planet's life. Was this mind which could penetrate others like a sword hopelessly self-deceived when it came to His own nature and person?

No one who embraces the lunatic view can handle this problem of the consequent discrepancy between His supposed mental derangement and His peerless ethical teaching. Anyone who accepts what He taught and believed about others is bound to accept what He taught and believed about Himself. The package of His teaching is all of a piece. It cannot be unravelled and construed as part brilliant and part deranged; part peerlessly good, and part hopelessly bad; part Jekyll and part Hyde. That might work on some human characters. It won't work on Jesus. No, not at all.

And those early followers perceived this with rapier-like clarity. They were not deluded about Jesus. They had seen the truth personified and knew it.

Chapter Twelve

RISEN INDEED

Christianity does not hold the resurrection to be one among many tenets of belief. Without faith in the resurrection there would be no Christianity at all.

Michael Green

After the Bolshevik revolution in Russia in 1917 a local communist lecturer was addressing a packed hall on the subject of the resurrection of Jesus. He spoke at great length, seeking to discredit it. At the end a Christian minister rose and asked if he might reply. He was told he could only have five minutes.

'Five seconds is all I need,' was his reply.

'You mean you can speak convincingly on the resurrection in five seconds?' asked the astonished lecturer.

'Indeed I can.'

The minister then turned to the audience and gave the traditional Easter greeting – '*Christos Aneste*'. (This is the Greek for 'Christ is risen'.)

The hall thundered back the traditional reply with passionate conviction, '*Alethos Aneste*'. (He is risen indeed!)

The lecturer knew he could not beat that sort of argument. A few verbal attacks on the central events of the Christian faith and indeed of all history will not disturb those for whom Christ has stepped out of the pages of history into the reality of personal experience.

But intellectual conviction and persuasion of the resurrection must normally precede personal experience.

St Paul, as he so often does, gives the right approach. In his letter to the Philippians he tells them of his ambition which was to 'know Him and the power of His resurrection' (Phil. 3:10).

Obviously his approach is not coldly academic. He does not want just to examine Christ, but to know Him. He doesn't want just to be persuaded of the resurrection, but to know its power in his own life. He is not simply after a religion, but a relationship. He is not just asking questions, he is involved in a quest.

And we have to be too. And in the process we shall beware, I trust, of that particular danger – all too evident nowadays when people face Jesus' resurrection – of accepting the most improbable natural explanations (e.g. collective hallucination, hypnotism of the unconsenting, conspiracy, lying and theft by otherwise good people, etc.) rather than admit the most obvious miraculous one.

Anyway, let's turn to historian Luke and see how he sums up the resurrection event. 'During the forty days after His crucifixion He appeared to the apostles from time to time, actually alive, and proved to them in many ways that it was really He Himself they were seeing' (Acts 1:3).

What do we have here?

A REAL DEATH

First of all, we have a real death. Luke says He was crucified. In his Gospel he says, 'He breathed His last' (23:46). All the other Gospel writers, as well as the first- and second-century secular historians referred to earlier, concur. He died. Moreover, He was pronounced dead by Pilate's soldiers who were skilled practitioners in death. Mark reports how Pilate 'wondered if He were already dead' (15:44) and then 'learned from the centurion that He was dead' (v. 45).

There is no suggestion in the text, nor anywhere else in the documents of antiquity, that He simply swooned on the cross, was removed before death, and then revived in the coolness of the tomb. Not only does that depart from the recorded facts, it requires us to believe that a shattered, excruciated, broken, bleeding, battered man could physically free himself from the grave-clothes, somehow roll back a stone of enormous weight and step from the tomb in semi-collapse to pretend to the world that He was the conqueror of death. Moreover this would have involved Him in conscious deception of the disciples, even had they been able to swallow such a story from such a broken wreck of a man.

Moreover it leaves us with a further problem. If Jesus didn't die when history says He died on the cross at Calvary, when did He die, under what circumstances, and why do we have no record of it?

REAL APPEARANCES

According to Luke, Jesus' very real death was also followed by very real appearances to the disciples.

Obviously these appearances were not some sort of trick, or that would land Je us, as we said above, in being party to brazen deceit.

Nor were the disciples seeing a ghost. In fact Luke tells us that when the ten first saw Him (Judas being dead and Thomas being absent) 'the whole group was terribly frightened, thinking they were seeing a ghost! "Why are you frightened?" Jesus asked. "Why do you doubt that it is really I? Look at my hands! Look at my feet! You can see that it is I, myself! Touch me and make sure that I am not a ghost! For ghosts don't have bodies, as you see that I do!"' (Luke 24:37-9).

And to dispel all doubt He then ate some fish with them!

Besides if they had been seeing a ghost or having hallucinations the body would still have been in the tomb for anyone to produce and thereby refute the whole resurrection idea.

Equally clearly this is no case of wish fulfilment for they were not expecting His resurrection and dismissed first reports of it as 'idle tales' (Luke 24:11).

NO FABRICATION

Clearly also this was no fabrication for they stood to gain nothing from such a fabrication except ostracism, persecution and death. No one puts his life on the line for a lie while at the same time preaching the primacy of truth! Besides this deception would have necessitated the theft of the body, and even had the disillusioned and shattered little crew been able to muster the courage, they could not have got past the temple guard (normally ten men) which had been placed deliberately at the tomb to prevent it from being tampered with (Matt. 27:65-6).

And beyond the guard was the seal (Matt. 27:66) to make doubly sure no easy fiddling could take place. The sealing process probably involved placing a cord across the stone with a formal Roman seal at each end of the rope. To break such a seal would incur the wrath of Roman law and thereby provide a further deterrent for would-be vandalisers. In any event Pilate's instruction regarding the tomb had been 'make it as secure as you can' (Matt. 27:65) and no doubt the Jewish authorities and temple guard had done just that.

A TRULY EMPTY TOMB

Now both friend and foe alike agreed and knew that the tomb was empty. The question focused on how it became so.

The initial story which the Jewish religious leaders told the soldiers to put out (i.e. a theft of the body by the disciples while the guards were asleep – Matt. 28:13) is so hopelessly implausible as to reveal just how desperate the authorities were to account for the empty tomb.

Apart from the fact that sleeping people can't testify to what has happened while they are unconscious, the hard reality is, as Jewish historian Alfred Edersheim underlines, that there was very tight discipline exercised over the temple police who would never have gone to sleep on duty. Or at least if one did, it is inconceivable that all ten would have! For one thing, the captain of the Temple, as he was called, made regular rounds of inspection during the night and the guards, who were not allowed to sit down, much less sleep, had to salute him in a particular manner. For another, any guard who had fallen asleep while on duty was beaten or his clothes set on fire. The Mishnah, the first-century collection of Jewish law, jurisprudence and ritual, confirms this as so.

Beyond that is the fact that the guards would never normally have expected the public to believe such a story. Everyone knew the guards would never so incriminate themselves unless they were in collusion with authorities who had already granted them immunity from criminal prosecution. The desperate story was a loser from the start.

If the friends of Christ couldn't have taken the body, the only other group who conceivably could have done so would have been the foes – Jewish or Roman or both. But the idea raises three unanswerable questions. Question one. What possible motive could they have had for doing so? Question two. Why did they not produce the body to collapse and terminate the resurrection preaching? Question three. What possible explanation can be given to the disciples' claim that they saw and touched and conversed with the risen Christ?

No. The foes of Christ didn't produce the body because they couldn't.

Nor, finally, had the disciples gone to the wrong tomb and then developed their message on the basis of a mistaken grave found empty.

I live in a little city called Pietermaritzburg which someone once described as half the size of New York cemetery and twice as dead! Well, New York cemetery is indeed large. But in Jerusalem they were not dealing with anything like New York cemetery but with a private tomb manifestly known to all involved in the strange saga of the death and burial of Jesus. And had the women and disciples all been so dim as to make such a mistake, Joseph of Arimathea, owner of the tomb, would have quickly set the record straight. It is also interesting to note that no one in those early years ever made the grave of Jesus into a place of pilgrimage. Why not? Because the grave was now incidental to the whole message of the risen Christ. Why go to the grave? He was no longer there.

The hard facts of the case show that the appearances of Jesus, about which historian Luke writes (Acts 1:3) cannot be explained as a trick, a ghostly apparition, a series of hallucinations, an orgy of wish fulfilment, or a catalogue of fabrication, deception or mistakes.

If these options are all non-starters, we are left with the overwhelming presumption that the story as narrated by the Gospel historians is true. Jesus rose from the dead and appeared to His disciples. Paul underlines this as so in his own chronicle of events (see 1 Cor. 15:3–9).

And of course we would expect any such appearances as those of which we speak to have a mighty impact on the lives of those who experienced them. And that is exactly what we find. The timid, frightened, disillusioned and shattered little band experiences something so titanic, so majestic, so overwhelming that they blaze through the Roman world like an unstoppable prairie fire. They know that a new day has dawned for the universe and for them and it is their task to proclaim it from the hilltops to all and sundry.

While a student in London I saw an advertisement in one of the London tube stations for an exclusive British newspaper. It described the newspaper as 'Read by an overwhelming minority'! This is exactly what the disciples became. An overwhelming minority. Nothing could stop them. Not the political might of Rome. Not the religious authority, tradition and scepticism of the Jews. Not the intellectual sophistication of the Greeks. Not their own physical fear, emotional timidity or intellectual limitation. They had seen their Lord alive, life had changed, and nothing could ever be the same again. They had good news and they would not keep quiet about it. When the authorities tried to stop Peter and John preaching some weeks later they replied, 'We cannot but speak of what we have seen and heard' (Acts 4:20).

PROVED IN MANY WAYS

Historian Luke says Jesus 'proved to them in many ways that it was really He himself they were seeing' (Acts 1:3). One translation says He presented Himself to them 'by many proofs'. The word used speaks of incontrovertible evidences. Against every instinct they were convinced. This happened through the appearances, through physical touch, through inner transformation in themselves and through active confirmation in their subsequent ministries. As they went out they found an undeniable power with them and, against all odds and in the face of enormous opposition, they grew and grew in number, with even many from the ranks of the Jewish priests becoming persuaded.

It is also noteworthy that the greatest initial success the resurrection preaching had was in Jerusalem itself, within quarter of an hour's walk of the grave for any who were sceptical. No one succeeds with a resurrection message while the decomposing body of the deceased lies a few hundred yards away!

Another illuminating detail about the first preaching bears notice. And this is the moment at which it started, i.e. forty days later. Historian Luke says that the preaching of the resurrection began not on the Monday following the resurrection, as one might have expected, but six weeks later. In fact no legend-monger would so have arranged the story as we have it in the Bible. Such fabricators would to be sure have had Jesus in Pilate's office on Monday morning to confound the poor fellow with casual comments on the rough weekend etc., thereby over-whelming him into a combination of both remorse and wonder! Beyond that, fabricators would also have had Jesus preaching in the synagogue and temple the following week to dumbfound the religious authorities and crush their scepticism with the irrefutable evidence of His physical presence!

Clearly no fabricator would arrange the story the way we have it. Equally clearly the disciples must have wanted to tell all and sundry right away about their Easter experience. But they didn't. Why not? Because, as the Biblical text says, Jesus told them not to. They had to 'wait', He said.

The fact is that the story is recorded that way because that is the way it happened.

THE CHURCH AND SABBATH

Another important evidence in this discussion is the early existence in our era of the Christian Church as a body of people united not so much around the teachings of Jesus as around the resurrection. This was the heart of the whole thing. You can explain Buddhism and Confucianism, as a consequence of the teachings of Buddha and Confucius respectively. But the early Church wasn't born out of the teachings of Jesus but out of His resurrection. As a Bach society needs the music of Bach not his dietary habits to explain its existence, seeing the society has his music and not his diet as its *raison d'être*, so the Church as 'the Jesus Society' needs His resurrection, not His teachings, to account for its existence seeing it was His resurrection and not His teachings which were primary, essential and foundational to their coming together at all as a group.

An equally significant sociological fact is the very odd development that the early Christians, a group of *Jews* for the most part, worshipped on the first and not the seventh day of the week.

Imagine in twentieth-century America, Britain or Australia trying to get the day of worship and rest moved from Sunday to Monday. It would require a phenomenon of quite massive proportions to produce that sociological effect. Even more so would this be true for Jews who were fanatically attached to their Sabbath on the seventh day.

The only satisfactory explanation is the resurrection of Jesus on the first and not the seventh day of the week!

VERDICT

We have gathered some of the strands of evidence together. Any single strand taken in isolation might just allow of some other explanation than the resurrection. But the explanation stands self-condemned unless it can account equally well for all the other strands. No other alternative than the resurrection fits all the facts and harmonises all the strands and data before us.

No wonder many who have legal minds and who are accustomed to weighing evidence have become convinced that Jesus really and truly rose from the dead.

We take one from the last century and two from our own. In a letter found after his death, Lord Lyndhurst (1772–1863), one of the greatest legal minds in British history, and attorney-general of Great Britain in 1824, wrote: 'I know pretty well what evidence is; and I tell you, such evidence as that for the Resurrection has never broken down yet.'

Stepping into the twentieth century, Sir Edward Clarke, a prominent British lawyer and one-time King's Counsel, writes to a friend, saying: 'As a lawyer I have made a prolonged study of the evidences for the events of the first

Easter day. To me the evidence is conclusive, and over and over again in the High Court I have secured the verdict on evidences not nearly so compelling.'[41]

Then there was Lord Darling, a former chief justice of England, who could affirm:

> The crux of the problem of whether Jesus was, or was not, what He proclaimed Himself to be, must surely depend upon the truth or otherwise of the resurrection. On that greatest point we are not merely asked to have faith. In its favour as a living truth there exists such overwhelming evidence, positive and negative, factual and circumstantial, that no intelligent jury in the world could fail to bring in a verdict that the resurrection story is true.[42]

THE VENTURE OF FAITH

All right, you concede, the data seems to say this astounding event did indeed take place in the past. But if I am to make the venture of faith, I must know whether this Christ who rose from the dead twenty centuries ago is still operative and at work today. Otherwise what possible point can there be in my trying to discover Him now?

Quite so. That is why we must now turn from the Jesus of history to the Christ of today.

Chapter Thirteen

THE CONTEMPORARY CHRIST

I am alive.

Jesus – Rev. 1:18

If you were ill and needed medical help it wouldn't take you long to decide not to go to a doctor whose remedies were known far and wide not to work.

It is also true in the spiritual realm. People don't want theoretical remedies of something which happened long ago. They want workable answers for now – today.

Now if the end of the story is that Jesus did in fact rise from the dead long ago as an item of history but His power is unworkable, unknowable and inoperable now, then an enquirer seeking a relevant day-to-day faith might well pack in the whole enquiry.

It is therefore in order to look at how Jesus, our contemporary Lord and Christ, can and does work in the present day in a wide variety of ways for those with eyes to see and hearts to apprehend. In this chapter we'll think of His contemporary workings in the spiritual realm of our lives and then in Chapter Fourteen we'll reflect on His workings in the physical realm of our lives.

HE TRANSFORMS LIVES TODAY

Beginning with the early disciples and Paul of Tarsus we

see this dramatic process at work as catalogued in earlier chapters. Paul sums up the happening he and others experienced, saying: 'When anyone becomes a Christian he becomes a brand-new person inside. He is not the same any more. A new life has begun' (2 Cor. 5:17).

A sign outside a second-hand shop once read, 'We can repair anything except a human soul'. The marvel of Christ and His power is that He can repair a human soul and He can change individual lives. To this we have already testified earlier with my own experience and that of Stephen Lungu.

Let me add two other examples. I think first of Alec Smith, son of former Rhodesian Prime Minister Ian Smith. For excessive drinking, heavy drug-taking and general bad behaviour he got himself expelled from Rhodes University in Grahamstown, South Africa. Then back in Rhodesia (as it then was) he got into trouble with the police for being a recipient of marijuana smuggled into Rhodesia from Mozambique. All this, of course, hit the newspapers in a big way.

One of the local churches in Salisbury (now Harare) decided to take Alec on as a sort of prayer project.

Day and night for weeks they focused prayer on this troubled young man.

The results of this Alec explained to me himself one night in my house when he visited us with an African friend, Arthur Kanodereka. Arthur, incidentally, was himself another marvellous example of spiritual transformation from hatred and violence to the love of Christ. Tragically Arthur was later blown up by a car bomb some months before Zimbabwean independence.

Alec told me his story as follows: 'I was driving along a road in Salisbury when I had a very distinct sense of an inner voice saying to me, "Pull to the side of the road." This I did at once. The same voice rang again in my soul, "Take up the New Testament and read it." That was that. I returned home at once and locked myself away for three days with a family Bible. During that time Jesus met me and changed my life.'

At the point in time of our discussion Alec, along with Arthur and others, was caught up in a powerful and loving labour of reconciliation in which they were serving as catalysts to dialogue between desperately polarised blacks and whites in pre-independence Zimbabwe. He had become a thoroughly transformed man by the contemporary power of Christ.

Another story which comes to mind is that of a businessman friend in our area. Alastair and his wife, Pearl, came to a study group in our home. One day in a quiet, undramatic manner, nothing like Alec's story, they said 'yes' to Jesus Christ. In the weeks and months and years following they have gone on from strength to strength in every way. They are today living demonstrations of a Christ who works, and changes lives and gives meaning where other things, such as money and success, invariably fail.

Yes, Jesus our contemporary changes our lives – dramatically or quietly – whether of those who have been in deep trouble or those who have been plodding along in a normal but meaningless way. He meets us in failure or success, in joy or in sorrow, in the normalities of daily life or in the freak situation.

No wonder the Bible says, 'When anyone becomes a Christian he becomes a brand new person inside' (2 Cor. 5:17).

HE REPAIRS RELATIONSHIPS TODAY

Pam Irish was my secretary for a number of years. Some years previously her marriage had been in a total shambles. In fact she and Anthony finally got divorced.

Then Christ came into her heart. Before long she felt a

great inner constraint to go to Anthony and ask
forgiveness for where she had contributed to the break-
down of the relationship. Anthony saw a whole new
dimension of humility, love and forgiveness in his wife
and wondered what could have brought this about. Pam
explained what Christ had done in her life.

This so affected Anthony that he was constrained to
investigate the claims and power of Christ for himself.
Glorious discovery followed which not only brought him
a new and humble flexibility as well, but love began to be
reborn in his heart for his wife. This led to their
'remarriage', as it were, and today they are both as happy
as sandpipers and in fact in full-time Christian work.

What power did this? I believe it was the transforming
power of the contemporary Christ.

I have seen this same reconciling power at work many
times between estranged parents and children, or between
alienated friends, or between black and white. It is a
mighty and very real thing.

HE GUIDES PEOPLE TODAY

The village in which I live is set in what is known in our
area as a 'mist belt'. This mist can become so thick at times
that visibility on the near-by freeway can be almost down
to zero. To cope with this our highway authorities have set
little reinforced glass 'cat's-eyes' down the centre line of
the highway. In fog this is a life-saver. In fact in the
thickest fog one can only see one cat's-eye ahead. But it is
enough. If you can see the next few yards, you are all right
and can reach your destination.

In the Christian life the sense of being shown just the
next 'cat's-eye' by a divine guiding hand is one of the most
real phenomena in Christian experience, and multitudes
in every age have been able to testify to the reality of it.
Although often very subtle, the way this happens is such
that people can look back over a lifetime and say, 'Yes, He

has shown me the way. He has indeed led me step by step.'

Isaiah 48:17 records, 'I am the Lord your God... who leads you in the way you should go.' Multitudes can say: 'Yes, that is true. God has done that for me.' The writer of Proverbs knew this truth and said: 'In all your ways acknowledge him and he will make straight your paths' (3:6).

In my own experience I can look back at so many points where I might have made a wrong or even catastrophic decision and can recollect seeking God's mind for direction. Various factors, counsel, circumstantial happenings, seemingly human insights or some sense of a word from the Bible would push me in direction A rather than direction B. Hindsight says, 'True to His word and promise, God was there guiding.'

While quiet and unspectacular guidance is the norm, occasionally people have very unusual and extraordinary experiences of the living, guiding power of Jesus.

Catherine Marshall tells that she has known many stories of people being delivered from death by hearing an inner word of guidance from the Spirit of God at a critical moment. She sees these as fulfilling certain Bible promises. For example Proverbs 1:33 says: 'Safe is he who listens to me: from fear of harm he shall be wholly free' (Moffatt translation). Or take Psalm 68:20, 'God is to us a God of deliverances and salvation, and to God, the Lord, belongs escape from death' (amplified translation).

Says Mrs Marshall:

Across the years I have heard so many true incidents of escape from death by following the Spirit's instructions that it is difficult to choose among them. All have this in common: someone in a crisis situation was able to hear the Spirit's quiet interior voice and moved to obey, thus escaping death.

One evening over dinner in a New York City restaurant a friend told this story... Several years previously she and her two young nephews were aboard a plane at Orly Airport (Paris) waiting to take off for London. 'As I sat there,' the friend told me, 'suddenly that quiet but very clear and authoritative Voice told me to take my nephews and deplane at once. No explanation was given. I obeyed and even managed to get our baggage pulled off.' She paused looking me directly in the eyes. 'That plane crashed. All aboard perished.'[43]

To me that speaks of the living God in action in the twentieth century. One wonders how many accidents and tragedies might be avoided if for example ground engineers, or pilots, or motorists or miners had ears sufficiently tuned to the living God to hear His whispers of caution, guidance or warning.

HE CREATES MIRACLE ATTITUDES TODAY

One mighty area Jesus works on in our lives is that of attitudes. A former secretary of our team in Zimbabwe told me how she and her husband were disturbed one night by sounds in their house. They went downstairs. As her husband got into the lounge, he was riddled with machine-gun fire from several guerrilla fighters who had penetrated the house. He fell dead at her feet in a pool of blood.

Mysteriously, the men did not kill her or her children. They did however talk Marxist propaganda to her for two hours over the dead body of her husband. Then they left.

But the real miracle to me was that she showed not a trace of bitterness towards any blacks and her spirit reflected the truly authentic Christian marks of forgiveness, love and grace.

Or again I recollect a man coming up to me in Washington DC and saying: 'I want to come to South Africa and share my testimony with whites. You see, I was the chief bomber of the Ku Klux Klan. I shot a policeman but fortunately did not kill him. He turned out to be a Christian and wounded as he was, and probably thinking he was dying, he shared Christ with me. Christ came into my heart and changed me completely. Now I deplore racial violence and love black people.'

Pretty amazing, isn't it?

HE ENABLES TODAY

Another very remarkable thing is that God enables us to do what He calls us to do and wants us to do. Many, many Christians will testify to the reality of feeling 'helped' and 'strengthened' in many situations which they would otherwise not have been able to handle.

In my own life I have used a sort of emergency verse thousands of times over when I felt God was asking me to do something I couldn't manage. The verse is Joshua 1:5, 'As I was with Moses, so I will be with you; I will not fail you or forsake you.' And truly I can say as my testimony over many years that God has been most marvellously faithful in never failing to help me and in not forsaking me when I was sure I would sink completely unless He came to my aid.

Much of this sort of enabling help takes place in unspectacular ways, although the sense of being helped and enabled is very real. However, there are special situations which need special enabling, and in some of those we may have the privilege of seeing God do a very special work of assistance.

My friend Os Guinness of Oxford reports one such experience, and very strange it was. He reports as follows:

Speaking once at Essex University, I saw sitting in the front row a strange-looking girl with an odd expression on her face. Remembering an incident the previous night when a radical had tried to disrupt the lecture, I spoke on but also prayed silently that she would create no trouble. She remained quiet the whole evening but came up as soon as it was finished with a very troubled look and asked what spell I had cast to keep her quiet. She told me she was part of a spiritist circle in the South of England and that the spirits had ordered her to travel to Essex, where she had never been before, to disrupt a series of lectures beginning that week. The curious sequel to this was that when I arrived back in Switzerland someone else in our community, far from a fanciful visionary, asked me what had happened in the Essex lectures. Praying for them one morning, *she had seen in a vision, as real as waking reality, the lecture hall and the strange girl about to disrupt the meeting.* Having prayed for her, she was convinced that nothing had happened, but she wondered if it was just her imagination. The presence of a Christian praying in the power of the Holy Spirit is always enough to render the occult inoperable.[44]

Os needed special help and enabling in that mysterious situation and so God led someone far away to pray very specially for him so that the spiritist power of an alien agent could not disrupt his lecture or block his freedom.

HE ENCOURAGES TODAY

This enabling work is quite closely related to another divine work – that of encouragement. It says of David in the Old Testament that 'he encouraged himself in the Lord' (1 Sam. 30:6). That's one way of doing it. We remind ourselves of God's power, promises and presence.

Moses likewise is told several times to 'encourage' Joshua (e.g. Deut. 1:38; 3:28). In other words he was to help him have courage. God always wants to encourage us, often through other people, and to have us encourage others.

Once when I was in Australia I was moving towards a particularly demanding assignment in the form of a mission to King's School in Paramatta, a suburb of Sydney. Not only was I feeling somewhat jaded from three weeks of on-the-go ministry in Melbourne, but I knew Aussie young people to be fairly formidable and 'tough', as they say, and besides that many had high expectations of this mission to the famous and distinguished King's

School – the oldest and largest private school in the country. Would I and could I manage?

Inevitably my knees began to knock and my normal butterflies were coming on strong, only this time they were flying in formation! I stepped off the plane in Sydney wondering what the week held, how I would cope and how I would find my way to Paramatta. 'Lord help!' my soul was saying.

Having a letter and some cards to post to my wife and children, I began hunting for a post-office. I tracked one down in the airport, only to find it closed. Next door stood the men's toilet to remind me that not only grace but nature has its calls. Exiting from the toilet moments later, I found a very gracious distinguished-looking gentleman opening the door for me. 'After you,' said he with a big smile, and followed me out.

I thanked him kindly and then said a little plaintively, 'Excuse me, sir, but do you know where I could get some stamps?' He apologised profusely that Australian post-offices were shut on Sunday, lamented he had no stamps on him and then asked where I was from ('Thy accent betrayeth thee!') and what I was doing in Sydney.

'I'm from South Africa,' I replied a little lamely, 'and I'm here to do a Christian mission in a big school called King's – in Paramatta. Have you ever heard of it?'

At this he almost popped! And so did I as he responded! 'Well I'm blowed,' he said. 'I've been associated with King's for forty-two years, though I've recently retired. I was a schoolboy there, I was chaplain of the senior school for years, and headmaster of the junior school for a long time. My name is Chum Price. King's has been my life. I've been on the staff there all my life. I probably know more about it than any man alive! Let me drive you to Paramatta, we'll have lunch in a café and I'll give you a full briefing and all the low-down on how to hook all those wild Aussie teenagers. Here's my wife. Let's go down to my car. We're free for the rest of the day to be at your disposal!'

The briefing, of course, was the best. By the time we parted I knew as much about King's School as any foreigner or visitor possibly could. But more than that, God had mightily encouraged me in my spirit, especially when I reflected on the human, mathematical odds (Sydney having 6 million people) against my meeting in an airport toilet with the one man on planet earth who could most help and encourage me with my daunting assignment.

From then on I believed it was truly God's will for me to be at King's School and He was going to stand by me with the strength and encouragement I needed. And He did!

Coincidence?

Another incident of supernatural encouragement came my way once when our African Enterprise team was facing a problem which came to a head on *Monday, July 11th, 1983*.

In November the executive of our International Council was to meet in Santa Barbara, California, close to Pasadena, the US headquarters of our work, to try and sort out the problem.

I arrived in Pasadena on a Friday night and received a message to phone a Mrs Peggy Rae. I had met Peggy and Philip Rae (a Baptist pastor) back in the early 60s when our team was getting started. Then they had vanished from contact until 1980 when I met them again at a conference. And in the nearly four years since then I had not seen them. So we were very out of touch and they were not even on our African Enterprise US mailing list.

'Michael,' said Peggy when she came on the phone, 'I've been wanting to get in touch with you because I have a message for you from the Lord. It came to me in a very vivid dream.'

Peggy then proceeded to elaborate a visual picture of our problem. An explanation of its dynamics followed, along with a clear elucidation, as given in the dream to her, of the line I needed to take in facing the situation. I took down forty points of incredible, mind-blowing detail.

I met her and her husband two days later. 'I can see your natural mind is rejecting all this,' Peggy said.

'Yes, it is, Peggy,' I said, 'It's too inexplicable. It would seem someone has briefed you in enormous detail on our work and on its current problem.'

'No one has briefed me, Michael. I know little or nothing of your work. I'm not even on your mailing list. I don't know your colleagues. And I've not shared the details before now of this dream with anyone, not even my husband.'

My conversation with Peggy and her husband went on for half a day. Towards the end of the time it occurred to me to track down when she had had the dream. A combined bit of detective work on this detail finally gave us the answer. I was stunned. The dream had come to her on Monday, July 11th – the very day our problem came to a head half a world away.

Peggy had been shown it all. Moreover the risen Jesus had given her an explanation plus instructions for me at the very same time as the problem was surfacing. Needless to say, her word encouraged me enormously.

If someone wants to argue all that as coincidence they are free to do so. But by my lights it is to stretch credulity to breaking-point. Far simpler is to see this as Jesus, our contemporary, living and acting in the here and now on behalf of His children and His work in the world. How He does it is up to Him. Whether by dream (as often happened in both Old and New Testaments) or by the sovereign arrangements of circumstances, or by seemingly very natural and normal processes of ordinary human thought, counsel or wisdom. But the fact is that He is alive and active. And one of the things He still does is to encourage His children in situations of trial, crisis, perplexity, or trauma. And why not? He is, after all, 'our Father in Heaven'.

All the preceding stories reflect, I believe, the activities of the risen Christ in the realm of our spiritual lives.

But does He ever act to protect, or heal or help in the realm of our physical lives?

Indeed He does.

Chapter Fourteen

HE HELPS AND HEALS

> Whither shall I go from thy Spirit? Or whither shall I flee from thy presence? If I ascend up into heaven, thou art there: If I make my bed in hell, thou art there. If I take the wings of the morning and dwell in the uttermost parts of the sea; Even there shall thy hand lead me, And thy right hand shall hold me.
>
> The Psalmist David – Ps. 139:7–10

If Jesus our contemporary acts to help us in our spiritual lives, He also does so in our physical lives. Thus He can protect us in physical danger, He can heal us in physical illness and He can help us in physical suffering and death.

HE PROTECTS TODAY

Both the Scriptures and life introduce us to the concept of a protecting God who is able to deliver His children out of situations of extreme danger, if that be His purpose and plan for that life at that moment.

Our Southern African subcontinent has, as the world well knows, been convulsed with political and military struggles for several decades. One of the most terrible was that which traumatised white and black Rhodesians in the twelve-year civil war leading up to Zimbabwe's independence.

Some amazing stories of divine protection have come out of that happening. Not that God *always* protects His people from danger or preserves them from premature death. But when it is His will to do so, then the manifest intervention of God will often be evident.

Earlier this year I visited Phil and Lynette Alexander (Lynette is the sister of my wife's brother-in-law – if you can conceive the connection!) to get their story first-hand.

Both Phil and Lynn had committed their lives to Christ not so very long before this incident and they had time and again entrusted their safety to God's protection. Living in Chipinga, not far from the Mozambique border, they were very vulnerable to guerrilla attacks and many in their area had experienced this horror. Numbers had died.

About 8.45 p.m. one night their house was riddled with many rounds of ammunition fired through the open doors and windows. The bullets also penetrated the flimsy wooden walls without difficulty. As Lynn sat on the floor of her bedroom cutting out a pattern, a hail of bullets screeched through the room all around her without one touching her. Phil and all the children were likewise spared in the other rooms. Most remarkably three bullets in direct line with the head of their sleeping baby failed to penetrate the last half-inch of wood, although everywhere else along that same wooden wall the bullets had effortlessly penetrated clean through.

'It wasn't our time,' said Phil, 'so God's protecting hand was over us. In fact,' he added, 'I had further evidence of this a little while later when I was driving a truck in convoy up to Umtali. At zero hour, when I could do nothing about it, I saw and felt my front wheel go over a little hole in the tarmac of the road. I went cold with the chill of horror and broke into a sweat. When we checked out the hole we found not only a land-mine but one reinforced by a very powerful mortar bomb. I had gone right over the detonator without it going off! Truly we owe our lives to God's intervening power and protection.'

Slightly different was the experience of one young

Christian soldier. Driving a vehicle loaded with troops he suddenly saw a land-mine explode inexplicably right in front of his vehicle about ten seconds before he would have gone over it. The vehicle and occupants were showered with debris but no one was hurt. An unseen power seemed to have exploded it before they went over it. The boy's mother was a mighty woman of prayer and had been laying hold on God constantly for her son's protection.

In another area two cars were travelling together in convoy on a lonely, dusty farm road, when suddenly a great gust of wind came up. It developed into a mighty whirlwind which forced the two cars to come to a halt. When the windstorm was over, and the cars were about to move off, the people in the front car spotted a land-mine just in front of them in the road. The whirlwind had exposed it. They removed it and travelled on in safety.

One African pastor, again in Zimbabwe, had an extraordinary experience. He himself believed it was a miraculous deliverance from death by burning. He was captured by guerrillas, tied to a tree and doused with paraffin. A match was lit but the liquid would not ignite. His captors then tried throwing diesoline over him, but again the match miraculously failed to set the human torch ablaze. So the desperate men poured a can of petrol over him, lit several matches, tossed them on to him and then fled in fear as the oil-soaked pastor remained unharmed!

HE HEALS TODAY

Now healing is a very mysterious thing. Sometimes God heals in answer to prayer, even when the ill or injured may have little faith themselves. Other times He stays healing. Or else He brings it about through medical science and skill whereby doctors and nurses set the stage with surgery or drugs for the body's own healing properties to go to work. At still other times, the greatest saints and soldiers of faith may seem abandoned to their illness and sufferings by an apparently indifferent God. More on that anon. But it is very mysterious, as I say.

However, in this little section I simply want to affirm one basic fact and that is that the healing power of Jesus, which we see so dramatically in the New Testament, is still evidenced in certain situations in the twentieth century.

One doctor, H. Richard Casdorph, in his book *The Miracles*, testifies to many cases of miraculous healing. He writes:

> I have documented these cases as accurately as possible, utilising my professional and academic background. By checking the available medical records or consulting the patients and physicians, I sought to determine several things: that the individual had the disease he or she reported; that the diagnosis had been made by a competent medical authority; and that the reputed healing had been verified by physical examination and, where necessary, by laboratory studies. Each person studied in this book continues in vigorous health at the time of this writing. Only one of their healings occurred less than a year prior to publication. The fact that physicians told several of these people that they had a fatal or incurable disease should not cast doubt on those doctors' competence. On the contrary, it should certify the serious nature of the healings. As a physician I attempted to document these stories as accurately and objectively as possible.[45]

Dr Casdorph then goes on to record some astonishing stories of God's supernatural power in healing. I lift out just the nub of one of these relating to a 45-year-old bank executive, Mr Ray Jackson, who had contracted cancer of the left kidney. This had then spread to other parts of his body. In spite of a kidney removal and a finger amputation, the cancer became evident in the groin, the pelvic bone, the breastbone, the sacroiliac joint, the lower leg bone and elsewhere and further surgery was out of the question. Reports Dr Casdorph, 'The only hope might be in hormone and radiation therapy.'[46]

However, after being prayed for in a healing service, Jackson's pains left him and he appeared to be healed.

A few weeks later he had regained his normal weight of 180 pounds and could report not having missed a day's work in the previous weeks. He later testified in these terms: 'The doctors gave me all the usual tests, X-rays, examinations, etc., and told me the results were very good.' The doctors then scheduled an appointment for him some months later. 'At that time,' reported Jackson, 'all tests, including a complete bone survey showed that new bone had filled in and all my bones were perfectly smooth in all tumour areas. My wife and doctor joined me in prayer, thanking Jesus for His blessing of healing. Periodic checks since then have continued to confirm that I am fully healed.'[47]

Dr Casdorph notes apropos of Ray Jackson's case that it is notable for the wealth of medical documentation on it available from the prestigious Duke University Medical Centre. In fact the X-ray department's report contains these sentences: 'Healing is noted of the previously described metastatic [i.e. cancerous] focus in the left ischium [pelvic bone]. No other metastatic foci can be identified.'[48] If you're medically minded and can understand medical technical language, the full statement can be read in note[49].

LILIAN CHUNGA

Let me add another incident out of several in my personal experience.

Although I do not profess any special healing gift (Jesus after all is the healer), nevertheless I have shaken off a fear of praying for people's healing. I know God may say 'Yes' or 'No' or 'Wait' to such prayers, but from time to time, even in the twentieth century, He says 'Yes'. The mystery of why healing seems so often to be denied is another subject. But let me tell you the story of Lilian Chunga.

I was conducting some meetings a couple of years ago in Malawi. At the end of one meeting I indicated that I, along with other Christian workers, would pray for the sick. Sixty or so people remained behind. We prayed both corporately and individually for the whole group.

Two nights later I indicated I would once again pray for those who were not well. An ebullient, sparkling well-dressed African woman stood to her feet and asked if she could share her experience before I prayed with those remaining behind. I said she could. She introduced herself as Lilian Chunga.

She proceeded to narrate how she had been suffering from very high blood pressure (220) to the point where her doctors were extremely worried about her. She had been taking extensive medication which had not helped her much.

However, following the time of prayer two nights previously she had felt quite different and believed that Jesus had healed her. I admit I was horrified when she triumphantly announced: 'I have even thrown away all my medication.' After all, the medical profession and modern medication are, I believe, still God's chief way in our time of bringing help, wholeness and healing to most people.

Later I said to Lilian: 'Really, do you think it was wise to throw out your medicines? You shouldn't do that till you have seen your doctor.'

'But I have seen my doctor today, and he says my blood pressure is down to 140 which is normal for someone my age.'

Two years later, on a return visit to Malawi, I saw Lilian looking more radiant, less overweight and in better health than ever. 'I have never looked back from that point,' she exulted. 'And I am busier and more active than ever. Praise God.'

Yes, Jesus is alive. And among the many things He still does is the physical work of healing!

But not always! Sometimes precious people, even

people of deep and real faith, are left to suffer. This is indeed a mystery. When that happens the contemporary Jesus does something possibly even more astonishing. He strengthens and sustains, even in suffering and death. His helping presence, if not His healing power, goes with us wherever we are.

HE STRENGTHENS TODAY

The mysterious helping presence of God, our contemporary, is perhaps just as miraculous as healing. Why relatively few seem to be healed I can't say. Maybe many factors and components go into the divine equation at this point. Certainly there is the overall and stubborn problem of evil plus the fallenness, unnaturalness and abnormality of the 'whole creation' (Rom. 8:22). There is also the basic lack of faith on this dimension in the twentieth-century church, and Jesus said, 'According to your faith be it unto you' (Matt. 9:29; cf. Matt. 17:19–20 AV). Maybe we don't see so much of God's healing activity because our twentieth-century mind-set is so basically sceptical.

One would also have to add that beyond all those factors there stand the sovereign purposes of a God who does everything 'according to the counsel of his own will' (Eph. 1:11).

In any event, for all of us there stands the fact that there is some illness or accident from which each of us whether young or old, will die in due course.

However, my point here is that Jesus still performs truly miraculous inner workings in so many people, enabling them to bear and cope with physical suffering and approaching death.

I remember the case of Alfred Venn, the younger brother (23 years of age) of my dear friend Garnet.

He contracted cancer of the bowel. Some of us prayed literally day and night for some weeks for Alf and became convinced he would be healed. But after an initial rally, which looked very spectacular at first, he relapsed and the dread disease began to run away with him. I was very shaken at the time – almost disillusioned. As I drove away from the Venn's home I remember saying, 'But Lord, I asked you to heal him.' Then came the clearest sense of an inner whisper from the Spirit of God: 'No, you didn't ask me to heal him. You asked me to heal him *completely*.' It was a strange experience, yet very vivid for me. And I saw it as truly so, and not just a faith cop-out or a face-saving rationalisation, that when God's children die and go to be with Him, that indeed is *complete* healing. No wonder the Psalmist can say, 'Precious in the sight of the Lord is the death of his saints' (Ps. 116:15).

However, my special point here is that I vividly recollect in those closing weeks of Alf Venn's life how he was so powerfully sustained by the mysterious presence of Christ that he was able creatively to come to terms with dying and actually become excited at the imminent prospect of meeting Christ face to face in the hereafter.

HE UPHOLDS TODAY

Then I think of Maria Tunstall, one of the loveliest and most beautiful people it has ever been my privilege to know. She too contracted cancer, though only in her early thirties. What a shock it was to all who knew her, most especially to her husband, Lee.

Imagine the mystification, the anguish, the bewilderment, the questionings. A poem helped Maria particularly.

> Lord, I ask more questions
> Than You ask.
> The ratio, I would suppose
> Is Ten to One.
> I ask:
> Why do You permit this anguish?
> How long can I endure it?

What possible purpose does it serve?
Have You forgotten to be gracious?
Have I wearied You?
Have I offended You?
Have you cast me off?
Where did I miss Your guidance?
When did I lose the way?
Do You see my utter despair?
YOU ask:
Are You trusting me?

In speaking of a ten-to-one ratio of questions from them to God, Lee and Maria were joining most of those who have been called to walk the royal road of suffering. Yet as they walked it, they did not walk in defeat, because their spiritual ears were able to hear that one great question from the responding heart of God – 'Are you trusting me?'

So although they questioned, as is only natural, they also trusted. Right to the very end. Right up until Maria died. And in that was victory. Says the Apostle John, 'This is the victory that overcomes the world – our faith' (1 John 5: 4).

How? Well, because faith is the only faculty man has which enables him to wait even into eternity for an answer to the questionings of life. Faith in God also knows that while there may not be a satisfactory answer NOW there will be a satisfactory answer THEN.

'NOW we see through a glass, darkly; but THEN face to face: NOW I know in part; but THEN I shall know even as also I am known' (1 Cor. 13:12 AV).

What Paul means is that our understanding now in the face of life's mysteries and sufferings is partial and incomplete. But one day when we see our Lord face to face all will be made clear.

I remember receiving a tape from Maria made just a little while before her death. It touched me deeply as it revealed both her marvellous ability to trust and her Lord's equally marvellous and merciful ability to sustain and strengthen.

On the tape she said:

When one goes through difficult times, it is very easy to start questioning and doubting God's ways and character and motives. One is tempted to ask: 'Does God care? Does He know what's happening? Is He still in control?' We have found the only way to counteract these doubts and questions is to *fill our minds with what the Scriptures say about God's character* and to hold on to the many promises in Scripture that He gives us. We have to remember that *infinite power ruled by infinite love* is the basic Biblical description of God's character.

In all of this we have become more childlike in our faith, more trusting. We do not have to have all the answers to all the why's. We are to hold our father's hand and trust that He knows what He is doing and He will take care of us.

Maria then related how she wrote down many of God's promises in a little notebook and went back to them again and again. For example Jesus says in Matthew 28:20 'I am with you always.'

Likewise St Paul: 'I am sure that neither death nor life... nor anything else in all creation, will be able to separate us from the love of God in Christ Jesus our Lord' (Rom. 8:38-9).

Maria went on:

This was a rock to us. Even when we could not understand His *hand*, we could always trust His *heart*. We have also reflected how a beautifully designed tapestry has an underside which looks ragged and where the pattern is not evident. However, from the top side one can see the whole picture. So in life, we have the underside view. But God has the top view. He sees the overall picture. He knows what He is doing.

After Maria had died, Lee told me of the incredible strength and peace Christ had given both to Maria and to him through this horrific experience. 'Michael,' he said in a long-distance call from California, 'God has blessed and touched me mightily in this whole thing and He feels so close.' What a triumph! Lee and Maria knew the God who still upholds His people in the twentieth century.

The Psalmist put it this way: 'Even when walking through the dark valley of death I will not be afraid, for you are close beside me, guarding, guiding all the way' (Ps. 23:4).

OUR TASK TO TRUST

While he was dying, David Watson, the British preacher-evangelist, wrote a book called *Fear No Evil*. He underlines there the vital importance of keeping Jesus central as the object and focus of faith. David testified that he found Him as real and present in the dark as He had been in the light.

He notes:

> God never promises to protect us from problems, only to help us in them. If we leave God out of the picture, those difficulties might so strip away our sense of security that we feel vulnerable, anxious and afraid. On the other hand, those same difficulties could drive us back to God and so strengthen our faith. We might feel just as vulnerable, but we have to trust God because there is really no alternative; and then we discover that God is with us in the dark as in the light, in pain as in joy. When I was going through a traumatic time in my life, a friend of mine said, 'You cannot trust God too much.'[50]

Quite so. We cannot trust God too much. And as we trust Him, even in the deepest and darkest valleys, we know He is there, and utterly true to the promises of His word in the Bible.

In one of the closing statements of this moving book David makes this fundamental Christian observation: 'God offers no promise to shield us from the evil of this fallen world. There is no immunity guaranteed from sickness, pain, sorrow or death. What he does pledge is his never-failing presence for those who have found him in Christ. Nothing can destroy that. Always he is with us.

And, in the long run, that is all we need to know.'[51]

The experiences of people such as Alf Venn, Maria Tunstall and David Watson underline that whether in living or whether in dying, Christian people find Jesus Christ to be their living, contemporary friend who acts and involves Himself in clear and recognisable ways with those who put their trust in Him.

Doesn't the thought of encountering and knowing such a Christ capture your imagination and draw you like a magnet to Him? If so, you must now pause at a very poignant place called Calvary.

Chapter Fifteen

GALLOWS ON THE SKYLINE

Jesus gave history a new beginning. In every land He is at home: everywhere men think His face is like their best face – and like God's face. His birthday is kept across the world. And His death-day has set a gallows against every city skyline.

George Buttrick

The major question now before us is not so much who Jesus is and whether He is alive, but rather, being who He was and is, as Son of God incarnate, why did He die the death of a criminal on the ancient world's most cruel gallows? Says an old song, 'Why did they nail Him to Calvary's tree, Why, tell me why, was He there?' To answer this is to find the key to both life and afterlife.

SOMETHING WRONG

The Genesis story sheds light on this. It reports that something went wrong for man and in him. There was a turning away from God which brought a change in man. Man, made in God's image turned at a certain time in history from God as his proper point of wholeness, meaning and relatedness.

And when he did this, he became something he

previously was not – namely a sinner, living in disruption and distance from his creator.

A student in a pre-Christmas exam once wrote over the last question, 'God alone knows the answer to this question. Merry Christmas.' When he got the paper back the professor had written: 'God gets an A. You get an F. Happy New Year!'

That sums it up. Morally and spiritually, man scored an F with God and has done so ever since.

Not that he became all bad. But he became spoiled goodness. He became the curious contradiction of a creature who enjoys being naughty yet who has one part of him not only morally recognising that naughtiness and feeling guilty for it, but approving the superior power or law which judges and punishes that naughtiness!

This faces us with not only the mystery of evil, but the mystery of goodness. Robert Louis Stevenson once observed that even in the brothel or on the scaffold men 'clutch to the remnants of virtue'.

I suppose most of us experience this sort of Jekyll-and-Hyde dimension of our own natures and behaviour. Said St Paul, 'When I want to do good, I don't, and when I try not to do wrong, I do it anyway' (Rom. 7:19).

In fact what we feel is that there is a sort of civil war going on in us between our good self and our unruly self.

Psychiatrists tell us that mental health depends on a conscious reconciliation of the warring parties within us. This involves seeing who I am in the dark side of my nature. I don't have to approve it, but I must see that it is there and accept that the shame I often feel is a real, true and important indicator of my need for something the Bible calls forgiveness.

There is a tombstone in a New York graveyard which carries the one word 'Forgiven'. No name. No date of birth or death. No other epitaph. Yet there is no single comment or commentary on a human life of greater consequence than that. To know we are forgiven by God, with the past obliterated is to know the ultimate blessing.

The late Bishop Stephen Neill of Oxford once said: 'True forgiveness is the only completely adequate method of putting the past back where it belongs – in the past . . .'[52] Beyond that, forgiveness frees us to live fully in the present and to be assured of a glorious eternal destiny beyond the grave.

However, to speak of forgiveness and its importance implies that man actually is genuinely guilty for moral and spiritual failure in breaking laws which he did not put there but which press in on his life as part of his daily moral experience. Facing this is often quite a problem for us.

One of my children once broke a camera flash of mine. How hard it was for her to admit the carelessness that had resulted in the breakage. It was Christmas Day next day and imagine how touched I was when my present from her had a card attached to it saying: 'Happy Christmas. Lots of love, Debs. PS. Sorry Daddy.'

In spite of the difficulty of it, she had mustered the insight, the will, the humility and the courage to ask for my forgiveness. And how gladly I gave it. In fact I ended up feeling more guilty myself for leaving the thing in a vulnerable place!

Facing guilt and seeking forgiveness is hard for all of us. But we have to do it. Especially and primarily with God.

And in this we are not just coping with guilt feelings, which some psychiatrist could remove, but with real guilt for breaking God's law.

Now guilt is a serious thing. And it is made even more serious when we face the person called Jesus of Nazareth. The fact is that He forces us to face the truth that serious as our bad actions and overt deeds often are, they do not show the whole extent of our guilt. In fact, Jesus redefines our guilt to make it far more extensive than we ever realised. This happens as He moves from our overt acts, such as murder, drunkenness, adultery, theft, etc., to the inner impulses of our thoughts. In fact, He forces us to acknowledge the sin and state of rebellion which much of the time lies hidden beneath the surface of our lives. This reveals a breadth and depth to our guilt which is staggering. In bringing us to the realisation that we are guilty even for the hidden thoughts and desires in our lives which violate His perfect standards, Jesus redefines the proportions of our guilt and creates for us a permanent state of crisis in this area.

That we are in fact guilty to this extent comes home to us if we try to live even twenty-four hours in a state of 100 per cent purity, integrity and charity. Thus St Paul can say, and accurately, 'All have sinned and come short of the glory of God' (Rom. 3:23).

Put differently we can say that we are all guilty.

Beyond that Jesus says that every betrayal, every offence, every infliction of suffering, every cruel thought or word, every judgmental attitude, although our neighbour may be the victim, is first and foremost sin against God. 'Against Thee, Thee only have I sinned,' lamented the Psalmist.

Now we can see our guilt as the terrifying problem it is, because in reality it is guilt before God.

The question therefore facing each person is this, 'What can I do about this sort of guilt?' The answer is startling. We can do precisely nothing. Absolutely nothing. The guilt is not before ourselves, or we could forgive ourselves. It is against God. There is therefore nothing, repeat nothing, which we can do about it. It stands there as an objective reality. We cannot solve it by losing ourselves in a hobby, taking a trip overseas, buying a yacht to amuse ourselves, getting lost in a book, becoming religious, or humanitarianly minded. We cannot even solve it by thinking positive thoughts or giving money to the Church. All we can do is thank God for what He has done.

DIVINE DILEMMA

Not that this was without problem or dilemma for God

Himself. While admitting the need for forgiveness is a major problem for man, the granting of it is in fact a far more major problem for God.

The dilemma for God arises out of His very nature as totally holy, totally just and of 'purer eyes than to behold iniquity' (Hab. 1:13). If God is the ultimate epitome of perfect holiness and perfect justice He cannot overlook or excuse man's waywardness, sin and rebellion.

Yet His perfect love and His unfathomable commitment to man call on His nature to forgive man.

The dilemma then is this – how can a loving God forgive human rebellion and moral waywardness and remain true to a holy nature implacably set against rebellion and waywardness? How can a God of holiness and love accept sinners and rebels without debasing the coinage of His holiness or sentimentalising His love into an immoral indifference to wrong?

The divine necessity is clearly not just to forgive, but to forgive in such a way as to show that God is irreconcilable to evil and can never treat it as less serious than it is.

It is easy to see how forgiveness at times can be more of a problem to the forgiver than the one seeking forgiveness when you think of a judge in court faced with a murderer who is deeply repentant and asking for the court's forgiveness. What is the judge, who represents law and justice, to do, especially if he is also a man of compassion?

Likewise, what was God to do bearing in mind not only His perfect justice and holiness but also His irrevocable love and commitment to man? You see the Scriptures picture God as having bound Himself hand and foot to man – as in covenant with Himself to get man back into relatedness with his God. By His covenant love for man God has become stuck with him! He cannot abandon him. His love will not allow it.

So here He is – faced with this unique creature who needs saving because of his degradation and vice and who is worth saving because of his dignity and value.

PENALTY PAYER

Love had to find a way. And it did. It was the way of the cross. The infinitely mysterious way of a gallows on a skyline.

It happened like this. Holiness and justice demanded consequence and penalty. Love demanded compassion and reprieve. The only way out was for justice to decree a penalty and for love to pay it. God's justice therefore decreed, 'The wages of sin is death' (Rom. 6:23). His love said, 'I will pay the penalty myself.' St Paul put it this way, 'In Christ God was reconciling the world to himself, not counting their trespasses against them' (2 Cor. 5:19). Elsewhere the Apostle writes, 'God showed His great love for us by sending Christ to die for us while we were still sinners' (Rom. 5:8).

The cross, you see, is God's answer to His own dilemma.

Imagine a traffic cop catching you for speeding. He turns out to be a personal friend. Suppose you ask him to forgive you. What a problem you create for him as the representative and the personalisation of justice! To forgive you involves him in a denial of who he is. He has to betray his essential nature as an officer of the law in order to let you off the hook. Here, as mentioned before, forgiveness is more of a problem to the forgiver than to the one seeking forgiveness. The only way for the cop to resolve the dictates of both his justice and his love towards you is by decreeing the penalty of £50 in his justice and then paying it himself in his love. And so having written out the speeding ticket, he then writes out a cheque – payable to the Magistrate's Court for £50. Likewise God in His justice condemned us to spiritual death and separation from Himself. He couldn't overlook sin. But in His love He came in Jesus to pay that very same penalty that in His justice He had decreed.

Now back to the traffic cop and your speeding fine. Your freedom comes as you accept both the penalty and the payment. Having faced the bad news, you then respond gratefully to the good news.

The cross thus becomes good news for bad people and it remains ever so. This is the meaning of grace. It is the story of unmerited favour. Thus while law says 'You sin, you pay', grace says 'You sin, I pay'. An old song says, 'Jesus paid it all, All to Him I owe.' It is true.

LAMB OF GOD

There are other related metaphors the Bible uses to try and explain what happened when Jesus died on the cross.

For example, John the Baptist, the great forerunner of Jesus, exclaimed when he saw Him, 'Behold the Lamb of God who takes away the sin of the world' (John 1:29). In saying this John was alerting the world to the whole sacrificial system of the Old Testament where the sacrificial offering, very often a lamb, would absorb the guilt of the sinner and pay the penalty of death. As the Old Testament lamb bore the penalty, so Jesus as the Lamb of God, a lamb without spot or blemish, also came to bear our guilt and the consequences of it.

Jesus, as the Lamb of God, absorbed in Himself the consequences of our sin.

SACRIFICIAL LOVER

Another related image is that of the sacrificial lover, the one who will sacrifice him or herself for the sake of the beloved one.

Thus Paul writes, 'God commendeth His love toward us, in that, while we were yet sinners, Christ died for us' (Rom. 5:8 AV).

Calvary was supremely an expression of love. If we want to know how much God loves us, Calvary gives the answer. He loves us to the very end.

This picture of sacrificial love is sometimes mirrored both in the behaviour of animals and man. Once there was a fire which swept across a farmyard. A mother hen and her chickens were right in its path. The mother hen saw quickly and clearly that she could not escape the flames, given the speed at which they were moving. So she nestled down over her chicks and the flames roared over her. Afterwards the scorched body of the mother hen was found, but the little chicks beneath her were still alive. In her instinctive love she had given herself so that the little chicks might live. This is sacrificial love.

During the last war a number of British prisoners of war were in a Japanese camp. One day a shovel went missing. The suspicious Japanese suspected mischief and said that unless the shovel was returned the entire group of men working in a particular work-party would be shot. The threat seemed real and the danger increased as nobody owned up. All of a sudden the British senior officer stepped forward. Moments later he was shot. Next day the missing shovel was found and it was quite clear that no one in the work-party had in fact stolen it. Imagine how deeply moved those fellow prisoners were to realise that their officer-in-charge had stepped forward, although in complete innocence, to sacrifice his life out of love for his men so that they might live.

Jesus, knowing himself that this would be the way He would walk, put it simply as he spoke of Himself as a shepherd who loved His sheep. Said He: 'The good shepherd lays down his life for the sheep' (John 10:11).

RANSOM

The ransom picture is another way by which Jesus described what He would do on the cross.

'I have come to give my life a ransom for many,' He said (Matt. 20:28). In other words, I have come to pay the price to free that which was enslaved and to find that which was lost.

In the first century, the ransom money was the sum paid to purchase the freedom of a slave. When man is lost, he is a slave and in bondage. When he is ransomed by Christ, he is set free to enjoy the spiritual liberty he longs for. Said Jesus: 'I have come to proclaim release to the captives . . . to set at liberty those who are oppressed' (Luke 4:18).

A friend of mine was captured in German-occupied France and imprisoned during the last war. The French Resistance decided to try and free him. At risk and cost to themselves they succeeded in doing so. They paid a price to release a captive. In a sense they were offering to risk their own lives to secure my friend's release from captivity.

All this and more Jesus did when He died on the cross and gave His life 'a ransom for many'.

SEARCHER FOR THE LOST

How many times, I wonder, have Alpine mountain guides sacrificed their lives while searching for some climber who had lost himself on some distant peak.

Jesus said, 'The Son of man came to seek and to save the lost' (Luke 19:10). The cross was the cost to Him of that search operation for lost human beings.

And lost indeed we are. At a conference attended by thousands of people a woman, trying to find a seminar room, came up to one of my colleagues and said, 'I'm lost.'

'Where do you want to go?' asked my colleague.

'I don't know!' came the plaintive response.

How like the human race! We have not only lost our way, but we don't even know where we are going.

But Jesus, as the One who made us, keeps searching after us and He will continue to do so, no matter what the personal price to Himself.

A little English boy once lost on the River Thames a toy

boat he had made. For days he kept up an agonised search for it. Finally one day he saw it for sale at 10 shillings in a little second-hand shop. 'But that's my boat,' said the little fellow.

However, to his great grief the shopkeeper announced that if he wanted the boat sufficiently badly, he would have to pay for it.

The little boy went home, took out most of his savings, and returned to the shop to buy back his lost boat. The boat was now doubly his – first by creation and then by purchase.

Thus has the God who loved us made us doubly His – first by creation, and then by costly search and purchase through Jesus' blood shed on Calvary's tree.

And it is a price which prevails and works no matter how lost or bad we feel ourselves to be. I once met a girl who had been a prostitute, and then most gloriously she was led into cleansing, forgiveness and new life in Christ. In Nicaragua I once prayed in prison for a man who had murdered eight people, five of them members of his own family. Yet what a joy and privilege it was to tell him that the blood of Jesus covered even him and was price enough to pay for all the desperate and hellish things he had done.

None of us can ever be so lost that the searching initiatives of Jesus cannot find us.

TESTATOR

My African name is Mojalifa. It is a name given me when I was a child by the Basuto people among whom we lived. The name means the 'first-born son and heir to the father's fortune' – which never ceased to amuse my father, seeing there was no fortune to inherit! But if there were, that fortune could not have become mine until the death of my father. Why? Well obviously there can be no legacy without the death of the testator. What is in a will only comes into effect when the person whose will it is dies.

Now see what the New Testament says. The writer to the Hebrews sees Jesus as the mediator and testator of a new will or covenant or testament. He is the one by whom man can receive a unique legacy – 'an eternal inheritance' (Heb. 9:15a). How does this legacy or inheritance become ours? It becomes ours through 'a death which has occurred' (Heb. 9:15b). 'For where a will is involved, the death of the one who made it must be established. For a will takes effect only at death, since it is not in force as long as the one who made it is alive'. (Heb. 9:16–17).

The death of Jesus thus made valid and operative a unique will, a new testament, a glorious legacy – the promise of eternal life to all who are children of God. Says the Apostle: 'It is the Spirit himself bearing witness with our spirit that we are the children of God, and if children, then *heirs*' (Rom. 8:16–17).

In Galatians 4:7 he puts it this way to those who have responded by faith to Christ's work on the cross: 'So through God, you are no longer a slave but a son, and if a son then an *heir*.' Peter exults in the same truth: 'By His great mercy we have been born anew to a living hope through the resurrection of Jesus Christ from the dead, and to an *inheritance* which is imperishable, undefiled, and unfading, kept in heaven for you' (1 Pet. 1:3–4).

You are potentially heir to a glorious inheritance. To claim it, you must become a son or a daughter of the Father. How this happens must now occupy our attention.

If our guilt is potentially gone, the penalty for our sin fully paid, the consequences of our waywardness fully borne, a search operation successfully completed and an eternal inheritance bequeathed to us, what does there remain for us to do?

The answer lies in the words of hymn writer Isaac Watts:

Were the whole realm of nature mine,

That were an offering far too small,
Love so amazing, so divine,
Demands my soul, my life, my all.

Quite so. But how do I do it?

Chapter Sixteen

WIND, WIND, BLOW ON ME

> Men can only reproduce human life, but the Holy Spirit
> gives new life from heaven; so don't be surprised at my
> statement that you must be born again! Just as you can
> hear the wind but can't tell where it comes from or
> where it will go next, so it is with the Spirit. We do not
> know on whom he will next bestow this life from
> heaven.
>
> Jesus – John 3:6-8

Recently I read a splendid book called *A Severe Mercy* by
Sheldon Vanauken. It is a powerful and almost classic
story of human love and the search for faith. How the
author struggled and yearned to believe!

Said he: 'I was excited, enthralled even, by the
intellectual challenge. I might not have admitted it, but I
was coming to love the Jesus that emerged from the New
Testament writings. I had impulses to fall on my knees
and reach out to Him.'[53]

Maybe that describes you.

Later on Vanauken saw the issues clearly. Jesus must be
Lord of all, or not Lord at all. He had to be given first
place. The surrender was to be complete. A choice was
required. Sheldon Vanauken chose to believe in God.

And each of us must likewise choose. There is a decision
involved. We cannot and must not for ever flee. God offers
eternal life and immortality to man, but it is not offered
automatically. It is offered conditionally. The condition is

a response of faith from us. We must believe. We must receive. We must choose. This is not a matter on which to procrastinate for we do not know what a day may bring forth.

Perhaps we should also note here in passing that the Biblical picture of judgment is not one of God trying arbitrarily to make up His perplexed mind what to do with us on the basis of whether our positive Brownie points score higher than our negative black marks. Rather, judgment Biblically pictured is a final revelation of choices already made by us in life. If we choose Christ, with Christ then we will be, both in time and in eternity. If we reject Him, our choice will be divinely respected. If we choose eternal life, then eternal life we shall have. If we reject it, as is our prerogative, then without it we shall both live and die.

Likewise, if the forgiveness offered by God is something we want, then we must take it. In fact, the cycle of pardon has to be completed by the guilty not the innocent party. If you offend me, and I forgive you, then you must accept and receive my forgiveness for the cycle of pardon to be appropriately completed. The converse is also true. The only thing for which there is no pardon is the rejection of pardon.

A prisoner in the Southern State of Tennessee was once sentenced to life imprisonment for a serious crime. His friends, however, felt there were extenuating circumstances. So they appealed to the Governor. To their delight a pardon was granted. However, the prisoner out of some stubborn and inexplicable perversity decided to reject the pardon.

The case went to the supreme court. The issue was this – if a pardon is rejected, does the sentence stand or fall? The verdict was that the sentence stood.

The man thus lived out his pathetic life in the unnecessary misery and bondage of prison. Spiritually, many do the same. What folly! What utter folly! How much better just to complete God's cycle of pardon by receiving in Christ the forgiveness He offers.

Perhaps we can summarise the response required of us with this ABCD outline.

We take these in turn.

A Stands for Something to Admit

The first requirement in Christian commitment is that we admit that all is not well with us and that we do have a real need. God requires of us the humility to admit this.

However, when we open our Bibles we find that the need, though possibly experienced in terms of meaninglessness, emptiness or lack of purpose, is actually and basically a need for forgiveness. All our other dislocations arise from this fundamental chasm between us and God. Our problem is separateness from God because of our sin.

This is our situation:

```
┌──────────┐        ┌──────────┐
│  Man     │        │  God     │
│ (Sinful) │        │ (Holy)   │
│          │ Chasm  │          │
└──────────┘        └──────────┘
```

If in stubborn pride we refuse to make this admission, then Christ can do little for us. Jesus spoke of one self-sufficient and self-righteous man who said, 'I thank God that I am not as the other men are' and of another who cried out, 'God be merciful to me a sinner'. Only the latter, said Jesus, could be forgiven.

So the first thing to admit is our need generally, then our need of forgiveness specifically and by extension our need of a forgiver or saviour who will do the forgiving.

B Stands for Something to Believe

We must believe that Jesus is the forgiver or saviour we have just admitted we need.

In other words, we must see Jesus as the proper object and focus of our faith. We are to believe that Jesus, rather than anyone or anything else, is the one we need and the one who has the answers for our lives both in time and eternity. Said Jesus simply, 'Believe in me' (John 14:1). Paul was equally uncomplicated: 'Believe in the Lord Jesus Christ and you will be saved' (Acts 16:31).

Lots of people have faith. But the Bible says that's not enough. Faith must be rightly focused. It must focus on and rest in Jesus Christ.

For example if you had appendicitis you could think of putting faith in a quack or in a trained surgeon. Faith itself is not enough. To believe in the quack will only cause complications. To believe in the surgeon will produce the solution. Nor does it matter whether the faith placed is shaky or powerful. The important thing is not the amount of faith but its direction. A little faith in a great surgeon will prevail where lots of faith in a quack won't. Likewise lots of faith in a piece of string won't prevail as you swing over a deep canyon. That would just be, as they say, jumping to a conclusion! But a little faith in a nylon rope will get you to the other side!

So you must see Jesus and only Jesus as the right, appropriate and availing focus for our faith. You must believe in Him.

There is no way to get to the other side of the chasm brought by sin, except through Jesus.

Figure A illustrates this situation where none of our human efforts (e.g. sincerity, good works, generosity, religion, morality, etc.) can bridge the chasm between sinful man and a holy God. St Paul underlines that this salvation is 'not because of works, lest any one should boast' (Eph. 2:9 and Rom. 3:20). On the other hand the grace of God as demonstrated in the cross (Eph. 2:8; Col. 2:13-14) does span the chasm (Figure B).

Jesus and His death on the cross open up the way to forgiveness for us. He is the forgiver and saviour we need. Believe this.

Human Efforts (Fig. A)

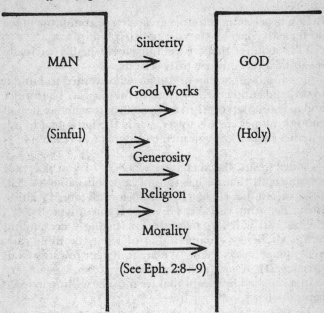

MAN

(Sinful)

Sincerity

Good Works

Generosity

Religion

Morality

(See Eph. 2:8—9)

GOD

(Holy)

The Cross of Christ (Fig. B)

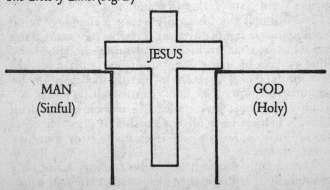

JESUS

MAN
(Sinful)

GOD
(Holy)

C Stands for Something to Consider

Before proceeding into this great step of commitment we do have to consider the cost of discipleship.

This requires that we ask ourselves whether we really mean business. Are we truly serious?

Jesus told a parable of a man who wanted to build a tower, and another who wished to wage a war. The former had to count the cost (Luke 14:28-30) as to whether he had enough money for his tower, while the latter had to ask whether he had enough men to win his war (Luke 14:31-32).

Added Jesus: 'So therefore, whoever of you does not renounce all that he has cannot be my disciple' (v. 33). Jesus meant that He had to come before all other loyalties. It is a daunting call. Yet He made it unequivocally.

This call will face us with a particularly demanding moral challenge – namely that of what the Bible calls 'repentance'. Says Paul: 'We are to repent towards God' (Acts 20:21). What did he mean?

In a nutshell he meant that we must be willing to leave behind what spoils our lives.

This word 'repent' is almost the very first recorded word of Jesus' public ministry. This comes in Mark 1:15. 'The Kingdom of God is at hand; repent, and believe in the gospel,' said Jesus to that first audience.

The original word basically means a change of mind leading to a change of direction. It is what the prodigal son did when he changed his mind about the imagined and illusory joys of living away from his father and then decided to change direction by leaving the life of the far country and going back home to the waiting father.

This repentance involves leaving or being willing with Christ's help to leave all known sins. It does not mean simply saying, 'Sorry God!' It means to stop doing the wrong things.

I heard Billy Graham once tell of taking a seat on a plane behind a thoroughly inebriated gentleman whose language, flirtation with the stewardesses and general behaviour were thoroughly embarrassing and offensive to everyone.

The desperate stewardess finally hit on an idea.

'Excuse me, sir, but do you know Billy Graham is sitting right behind you?'

'Well, I never,' said the delinquent staggering to his feet. Then holding out an unsteady hand he wobbled to Dr Graham and burbled out: 'Dr Graham, your sermons have really helped me!'

'Guess he didn't get the bit about repentance,' chuckled Billy as he told the story.

Quite so, because repentance involves changing the way we live and behave where aspects of our life and behaviour are not in line with God's standards.

There was a saying among ancient rabbis: 'If a man has an unclean thing in his hands, he may wash them in all the seas of the world and he will never be clean: but if he throws the unclean thing away, a little water will suffice.'

We are obliged therefore to throw away the unclean thing. Are we willing to do this?

This is something vitally important to consider.

D Stands for Something to DO

There are several aspects to what we must do.

1. *Choose Jesus as the Centre of your Life and as your Saviour from Sin*

The matter of final choice and decision is upon us. We are free now to make an unprogrammed, non-determined choice. And part of that 'Something to DO' is to make that choice. God wants to enjoy for ever the fellowship of free spirits which have freely chosen to live in that fellowship with Him. Indeed, the essential business of faith is the transference of our centre of interest and concern from ourselves to God. Although this choice and decision may involve a leap of sorts, it is not a blind or irrational leap. It is just that in leaping we do not know ahead of time exactly where we shall land or what will follow once we've landed! That's what makes it all such an exciting adventure. It is a leap in the light. Not a leap in the dark.

This is not to deny that some commitments and conversions may be more gradual and without a sudden leap. While my own conversion experience was a crisis at the end of a process, my wife's was all process. She can't remember when Christ was not real to her. For others conversion may happen, as with Saul, in a sudden right-about turn. Peter on the other hand came to Christ in fits and starts. The timing and way we turn doesn't matter so much as the fact of turning.

When finally by choice we cross that threshold and take Him as our Saviour, God 'justifies' us (or pronounces us innocent) in a single instantaneous divine act (Rom. 3:24, 28). And at that moment our 'names are written in heaven' (Luke 10:20). At that moment, whether we realise it or not, we are 'delivered... from the dominion of darkness and transferred... to the Kingdom of his beloved Son, in whom we have redemption, the forgiveness of sins' (Col. 1:13-14).

This miracle of being accepted by God takes place when we look to the Cross of Jesus, recognise Him as dying there for us, and then choose Him as the centre and Saviour of our lives.

Said Joshua in the Old Testament, 'Choose this day whom you will serve' (Josh. 24:15).

2. *Surrender to Jesus Christ as Lord and King*
A second aspect of response under D for 'Something to DO' is that we need to surrender our wills and destiny to Jesus Christ as Lord, King and Master.

One Christian of bygone times once affirmed in prayer,

'I am Thine – by purchase – by conquest – and by self-surrender.'

In my own case, as a young person, I had done everything in the religious life except hand over that stubborn will of mine and yield myself fully to Christ.

This handing over of the will and surrender of the self is basically an act of TRUST.

The other day I was crossing the rapids of a swollen river with my children. At several places my ten-year-old felt she couldn't manage.

'On to my back, darling,' I called out above the rushing water.

And up she clambered. Her trust had to be complete if she was to get across the torrent. If she'd kept one foot on a secure rock, or clutched to a branch behind her, we could have made no progress. But, no, she committed her whole self and all her weight and life and destiny to me. Not as a blind act of faith, but as a calculated act based on what she had come to believe of my reliability, nature and strength.

With Jesus, too, there can be no half-way houses. No partial response. The full weight of our temporal lives and eternal destinies must be committed to Him. We have to say: 'Jesus I surrender my life and destiny to you. I give you full control of my life. I make you Lord and King of my life.'

Bodies Too

This surrender will involve something else. St Paul calls it 'presenting our bodies to Jesus as a living sacrifice' (see Rom. 12:1). Obviously if we present our bodies to Jesus Christ we present everything inside those bodies. We present whom we are. Therefore, we present our *minds* to Him so that they may be used in Christ's service. We present our *hearts* so that He may express His compassion through them to the world. We present our *feet* so that Jesus may walk to places of need. We present our *hands* so that we may hold a spade, a surgeon's knife, a pen or a broom for Him. We present our *sex organs* to be kept under His control for the proper expressions of love or acts of procreation according to His purposes and His plan in the marital context. We present our *mouths* so that we speak for Him. We present our *ears* so that we may listen to the cries of a broken humanity. We will no longer be our own. We are presented to Him as a living sacrifice.

Not only do we present what we are, but *we present all we have*. A friend of mine once had the opportunity of sharing Christ with a big shipping magnate. The man was very touched.

Suddenly with a sort of rush of blood to the head, he blurted out, 'Do you think Jesus would like me to give Him a ship?'

My friend thought a moment – and then responded: 'No, I don't think Jesus wants you to give Him a ship. He wants you to give Him yourself.'

The shipping magnate reflected a look which mixed relief with apprehension.

Then my friend added: 'But of course Jesus knows that if he gets you, why, He gets *all* the ships!'

Commitment to Christ involves that sort of full and complete presentation of all that we are and all that we have.

3. *Open the Door of your Heart to Jesus Christ and Receive Him into your life in the Person of the Holy Spirit*
This opening and receiving is the final dimension of response under D for 'Something to DO'.

Back in 1955 at university when my friend Robert Footner shared Christ with me so clearly and decisively, the Scripture he used came from the last book of the Bible where the risen Christ says: 'I stand at the door and knock; if anyone hears my voice and opens the door, I will come in' (Rev. 3:20). That's His promise. We open the door of our heart, and He comes in.

While in Oxford in 1980 I visited Keble College chapel, which houses the famous painting called *Light of the World* by Holman Hunt. It depicts Jesus knocking on the door.

Apparently when the picture was first displayed, someone said to Holman Hunt: 'But you've forgotten something. There is no handle on the door.'

'Ah no!' replied Hunt. 'That's no mistake. You see, the door of our hearts which Jesus knocks on has no handle on the outside. Only on the inside. Because it is we who must open up to Him from the inside.'

Basically this is an act of receiving Him into our lives, as we would receive any friend who wanted to come close to us.

HOLY SPIRIT

Perhaps to be even more Biblically accurate at this point we should say that we receive the 'Spirit of Jesus' (Acts 16:7), otherwise spoken of in the New Testament as the Holy Spirit. In other words we receive Jesus in the person of His Holy Spirit.

Coming to the end of his sermon on the Day of Pentecost, Peter tells his listeners what response is required of them, 'Repent and be baptised every one of you in the name of Jesus Christ' (Acts 2:38). Then he indicates to them what two gifts will follow these acts of repentance and faith. The first is that they will receive 'the forgiveness of sins'. The second is put this way, 'You shall receive the gift of the Holy Spirit' (Acts 2:38). These are two astonishing Gospel offers which minister to the deepest possible needs of the human heart. God offers us on the one hand forgiveness for the past and on the other hand the possibility of being indwelt by Him in the person of His Spirit so that we go through life not alone nor empty but rather strengthened, comforted and empowered by His presence within.

NEW BIRTH

In a conversation with Nicodemus, a Jewish theologian, Jesus likened the Holy Spirit to the mysterious, invisible wind (John 3:8). That being so, we need to pray in the words of the Gospel song, 'Wind, wind, blow on me.' Solomon's worldly search, like a chasing of the wind, got him nowhere. For Jesus, in glorious contrast, the key to everything lies in allowing the wind of the Holy Spirit to blow upon us and indwell us and regenerate us into new creations.

This happens through what the Bible calls a new birth. When Jesus told Nicodemus that he needed to be born again (John 3:3 and 8) he said that the agent which would bring about his new birth would be the Holy Spirit. He told Nicodemus that he needed to be 'born of the Spirit' (John 3:6 and 8). Like the mysterious wind, the Holy Spirit of Jesus would come and do His regenerating and renewing work in the human heart. Like us, Nicodemus was being called to Jesus and to His Spirit.

In sum we could observe that our spiritual response involves *God the Father, God the Son,* and *God the Holy Spirit.* Paul said he preached 'repentance to God and faith in our Lord Jesus Christ' (Acts 20:21b), while Peter on the day of Pentecost said responding people should and would 'receive the gift of the Holy Spirit' (Acts 2:38). Thus we *repent towards God the Father* (Acts 20:21a). *We believe in God the Son* (Acts 20:21b) and *we receive God the Holy Spirit* into our hearts (Acts 2:38).

Or to use our *ABCD* summary again:

1. We Admit to God the Father our need. Our need of forgiveness and our need of a Saviour.
2. We Believe that Jesus the Son is the Saviour we need.
3. We Consider the cost and resolve to proceed into commitment.
4. We Do by an act of the will take the following steps:

- We choose Jesus as the centre of life and as our Saviour from sin.
- We surrender our wills to Him as Lord and King.
- We open the doors of our hearts to Him and receive Him into our lives in the person of His Holy Spirit.

COMMITMENT

So now I must at last put life's greatest and most momentous question to you.

Will you respond to Jesus Christ as Lord and Saviour and Friend and give your life in surrender to Him?

If you will, I should like you to find a quiet place, perhaps even right now, where you can be totally alone and undisturbed so that you may say a true and deep prayer of commitment along these lines:

Lord God and heavenly Father,
I admit to you my need, my need of forgiveness and my need of a Saviour.
And I believe that Jesus is the Saviour I have just admitted I need.
Moreover I have considered the cost and I am deeply serious in this response.
I therefore confess to you that I have indeed sinned against you in thought and word and deed and I am not worthy to be called your child.
But I do now want to turn from my sins and put them behind me.

This being so, *I come to you Lord Jesus* and affirm my belief in you as God the Son.
I take you and trust you as my own Saviour from sin through your death on the cross.
I surrender to you as my Lord and master and hand over to you the full control of my life.
I open to you the door of my heart and I ask you to come in in the person of your Holy Spirit as my closest friend and companion.

Holy Spirit of Jesus I receive you into my heart by faith.
Wind of the Spirit, blow on me. I call you into my heart to take
  over my life, to grant me a fresh start and a new birth. Please
  empower me for Christian living throughout the future.

And so Father, Son and Holy Spirit, I promise to serve you in
  my home, among my friends, and in your Church.
In the name of Jesus Christ I pray.

                                                    Amen.

Chapter Seventeen

FORWARD MARCH

> Every Christian is called to a clear and dedicated discipleship, whatever the personal cost may be.
>
> David Watson

It is a tremendous thing to take the step of commitment, faith and surrender of which we have just spoken. It launches one out on a brand-new life from which there is no discharge. So we cannot allow any wobbles of indecision or second thoughts.

After making a major decision, a politician said to his aide: 'About that charge that I'm indecisive. Do you think I should answer it ... or let it go ... or answer it in part ... or what?'

Well, that's no good! If you've come to this decision about Christ then press on decisively and with all resolution. Don't have second thoughts. Move on. For you are embarked on a lifelong adventure of discipleship, service, and growth involving every conceivable type of experience – some exciting, some dull, some happy, some sad, some extremely difficult, some joyful beyond the telling.

The original Greek word for follow is tied in with the same root word which we translate as disciple or discipleship. To be a disciple is to be a follower. Jesus said very simply to those first men and women who turned to Him, 'Follow me' (John 1:43). Now He didn't say they would necessarily have some big emotional experience. They were simply told to follow Him as an act and decision of the will. Of course, along the way they undoubtedly had some deeply emotional experiences which would have moved them to the very depths of their being. But their emotions were not the significant thing. Their decision to follow Jesus was what really mattered.

It is true today that many people want to come to Christ to have a sort of emotional trip or simply to acquire peace, joy and satisfaction. Some even see Jesus as the way to business success, financial prosperity or even perpetual health. But I do not see those blessings as either primary or prominent in the New Testament picture. It is true our Lord does bless His people in all sorts of ways, but the blessings are also mixed with experiences of trial and hardship which train and discipline us and which are often hard to handle. But these experiences are used by God to develop us. The writer to the Hebrews thus notes, 'For the moment all discipline seems painful rather than pleasant; but later it yields the peaceful fruit of righteousness to those who have been trained by it' (Heb. 12:11). Likewise James writes in his letter, 'Count it all joy, my brethren, when you meet various trials, for you know that the testing of your faith produces steadfastness' (James 1:2–3).

ASSURANCE

Because Christian commitment can often be followed by quite severe difficulties or trials, it is essential to understand that our commitment to Christ and our assurance of His commitment to us do not depend upon how we feel. We must therefore stand on the promises of the Word of God rather than on what our own emotions may or may not say.

Thus, for example, the risen Christ has given us the promise, 'I stand at the door and knock; if anyone hears my voice and opens the door, I will come in' (Rev. 3:20). Now that promise stands. It does not depend upon how we feel but on the committed word and promise of Jesus Himself. He says in effect, 'If you have truly opened the door of your life to me and asked me to come in through my Holy Spirit, then stand assured that I have come in, on the basis of my promise, regardless of how you feel.' This is what Christian people often call assurance of salvation. It is the assurance that Jesus keeps His word. Likewise Jesus can say, 'He who comes to me I will never cast out' (John 6:37). What a magnificent promise! Believe it! Claim it! Stand on it!

Then grasp the glorious related truth that God is never going to let you be separated from His love. Not by anything.

St Paul captures this magnificently in his letter to the beleagured believers in Rome: 'For I am sure that neither death, nor life, nor angels, nor principalities, nor things present, nor things to come, nor powers, nor height, nor depth, nor anything else in all creation, will be able to separate us from the love of God in Christ Jesus our Lord' (Rom. 8:38-9). It is really more than the mind can take in, but it's true! Once we have truly come to Christ nothing at all can separate us from His love. Absolutely nothing.

FOCUS ON FACTS

Nor should you allow anything to make you doubt the reality or seriousness of the step you have taken.

Let me illustrate. Imagine three little men walking along a wall. The one in front is called *Facts*, the one in the middle is called *Faith*, and the one at the back is called *Feelings*. While *Faith* walks along the wall looking at *Facts* he is stable, steady, and secure. But when he looks over his shoulder at that precarious and unpredictable character, *Feelings*, he is likely to stumble, totter, and maybe even fall off the wall. But if he keeps his eyes fixed on *Facts* he stays in good shape. And there are three facts in particular upon which faith concentrates.

The first is the historical fact of Jesus and His resurrection. The second is the Biblical fact of His promise to come into our hearts when we ask Him. The third is the contemporary fact that you have indeed asked Him to do just that. Nothing can alter those facts. If you heard tomorrow that the Third World War had broken out, that you had a chronic disease, and that a friend or relative had been killed in a car accident, your emotions would plummet to the very depths. But the three facts mentioned above would not alter. Regardless of your plummeting feelings, your faith stands secure, assured and settled because it is based on facts.

POWER FOR PROGRESS

Not surprisingly, the challenge of moving forward and making spiritual progress cannot be long delayed. And many will feel almost overwhelmed and discouraged at the prospect. They feel doomed to failure. 'I won't be able to keep it up,' they say. A British MP who committed his life to Christ expressed this kind of fear to Billy Graham. Dr Graham proceeded to give him a Bible and wrote a verse in the front: 'I'm confident of this very thing that He [i.e. Jesus] who has begun the good work in you will finish it' (Phil. 1:6). Yes, Jesus finishes the work He has begun in us and He does this by the power of His Holy Spirit.

Thus can Paul underline to the not very successful Corinthians that they actually have the Holy Spirit WITHIN them as the power needed to live the Christian life. 'You are God's temple and God's Spirit dwells in you' (1 Cor. 3:16). He is saying in effect, 'Seeing you have this power, use it!'

This is vital to grasp. We are not left to walk alone. Jesus walks with us and will live out His life in us as by faith we allow Him to do so (see Gal. 2:20).

Not that the disciple can stand back and do nothing. There are a number of vital disciplines which must be embraced if we would grow.

READ THE BIBLE

The first is regular reading of the Bible, even if only for a few minutes a day.

Writing to his young son in the faith, Timothy, Paul tells him that he is thankful that Timothy has from childhood been acquainted with the Scriptures which 'are able to instruct you for salvation through faith in Christ Jesus'. In other words, the Scriptures give us the instructions and information we need in terms of everything involved in finding our salvation and working it out.

This being the case, none of us can afford to do without a regular diet of the Scriptures.

A little child once wanted to give her father a Bible for Christmas. But she didn't know how to inscribe it. So she went into her father's study and looked around at the books on his shelf. Finally she found one which was inscribed and she presumed that this was the appropriate inscription for any gift book. So she wrote the inscription inside the flap of the Bible, wrapped it up in gay Christmas paper, and then finally presented it to her father on Christmas day. Imagine both his delight and perhaps his shock as he opened the beautiful Bible and read the inscription inside, 'With the compliments of the Author!'

The Bible does indeed come to us with the compliments of the Author and it is encumbent upon us to receive it as such, accord it that authority and seek to live by it in every way. A Chinese student in London once wrote home to his family in China after he had become a Christian and said, 'I am reading the Bible and behaving it.' That is what is required of each of us.

So acquire a modern version of the Bible and perhaps

some daily Bible study notes (for example, those put out by
Scripture Union whose address your minister would give
you), and begin to read the Word of God daily. You'll
never regret it.

PRAY

To cultivate a habit of regular prayer, even a short time
daily, is absolutely vital. This has been found down the
ages to be an indispensable Christian discipline. In this
regard it is better not to set some extravagant target and
never achieve it, but rather to aim initially at five or six
minutes a day and achieve it. Then build up the time as
you are able. But a brief time of quiet at the beginning and
end of each day is a magnificent discipline which will
repay enormous spiritual dividends in the life of anyone
who conscientiously pursues it.

I have personally found it helpful to use some form of
prayer diary which may be either something like John
Baillie's *Diary of Private Prayer*, which any Christian
bookshop could order for you, or else a three-ring binder
or notebook in which you can record things and people
you want to pray for. You can also take down notes and
insights from your Bible study. I like to use both these
tools and have found them in different ways to be
exceedingly useful.

In any event the important thing is that we persevere in
prayer so that our relationship with the living God may
deepen and grow.

Of course, we also have the joyful privilege of constantly
having God's ear, so we can converse with Him
throughout the day and not just in those special times of
quiet.

GO TO CHURCH

After a mission to a school a boy once said to me, 'But, sir,

you don't expect me to go to Church, do you, and be part of
that bunch of fuddy-duddies in our town.'

'Absolutely, young man,' I replied with all conviction.
'You must worship regularly with other Christians
because you need them and they need you. Maybe you
think they are weak. But if picked for your school rugby
team, you wouldn't withdraw just because it was weak
that year, would you? You'd pitch in and play harder than
ever – because you were needed more than ever. Likewise
the Church needs you and you need it. You need the help
of other believers more than you know.'

I took this line with one particularly bumptious young
man who continued to look sceptical. So I added: 'I know
your problem. You are looking for a perfect Church. But
you'll never find one. And if you do, it won't be perfect
after you join it!'

Beyond that, of course, stands the Biblical teaching of
the inter-relatedness of all Christian believers. We belong
together as a body (1 Cor. 12). So an isolated Christian is a
contradiction in terms. One person said he wasn't a pillar
of the Church, but rather a buttress because he supported it
from outside! But actually that won't do. Our involvement, if we would be true to our Lord, must be from the
inside as an actively involved participant.

In regular Sunday worship you will also receive the
sacraments, worship, pray, praise and receive instruction
and inspiration. The local church is where you will grow
through fellowship with other believers and where you
will develop both the gifts and the opportunities for
witness, service and mission. It is also a place where your
children, if you are a married person, can receive teaching
in Sunday school which will stay with them all their days.

No Christian can stand aside from the Church generally
or a local congregation specifically, for such involvement
is a vital part of God's armour for each believer.

SHARE YOUR FAITH

The Gospel is not something which we can sit down and privately enjoy for ourselves. We must be willing to share it.

All the Gospels record that Jesus' final words to His disciples were that they should go out and share the message of forgiveness and new life with all the world. This is not calling each of us to be some sort of tub-thumping evangelist nor does it oblige us to ask every person we meet whether they are 'saved' or not, which usually produces more offence than anything else. Rather it means that we are to be ever ready and on the alert to be open about our faith with other people so that they too may be helped towards a discovery of Jesus Christ. In fact, a secret disciple is a contradiction in terms. Either our secrecy will destroy our discipleship or our discipleship will destroy our secrecy. Obviously it must be the latter. We cannot be secret disciples. We must be willing to share our faith in whatever way is easy and natural for us with others.

When I was a student a certain Major Batt was a popular speaker on the university circuit. He had been won to Christ towards the end of the war and had become a radiant witness and a powerful testimony to his Lord.

I once heard him tell the story that not long after the war ended he had a dream. In his dream he was standing in the presence of Jesus Christ in eternity. It was marvellous, thrilling and ecstatic to stand face to face with the Lord he had loved and served in life. But after the initial moments of adoration and wonder, the Saviour said to him 'Turn around.' In his dream, Major Batt turned round. As he did so he saw a vast and limitless sea of faces. It was indeed, as the Bible says, the number of the redeemed, a number which no man can number, a thousand times ten thousand and thousands of thousands.

As he stood looking he heard the voice of Jesus behind

him, saying, 'Can you see anyone who is there because of you?'

Major Batt reported how he searched, scanned and scrutinised the immense throng to see if there was anybody who was in heaven as a result of his testimony and witness. But he was not able to see a single one.

He awoke almost in a cold sweat, but with the resolution now placed irrevocably upon his life that he would seek wherever possible and wherever appropriate to be a forthright, courageous and sensitive witness for his Lord.

Truly Major Batt had heeded Jesus' simple words, 'You shall be my witnesses' (Acts 1:8). And each of us must do the same.

OFFER YOUR GIFTS AND SKILLS

In a remarkable section of his first letter to the Corinthians St Paul tells them that through the Holy Spirit each of them has been equipped with certain gifts, endowments or capabilities to enable them to serve the living God. Says the Apostle: 'There are varieties of gifts, but the same Spirit: and there are varieties of service, but the same Lord: and there are varieties of working, but it is the same God who inspires them all in every one. To each is given the manifestation of the Spirit for the common good' (1 Cor. 12: 4-7).

In other words, everyone has a contribution to make and is given by the Spirit of God the divine ability and capability of fulfilling that contribution. Some people are given the ability to teach or preach or lead. Others are enabled to do administration, handle finances, give generously of their means or else perhaps just help in a variety of seemingly modest ways in the life of the Church and in their relationships with people round them. Paul spells all of this out in a number of different chapters, two of the most prominent being 1 Corinthians 12 and 14. But the exciting thing here is that every single person is given an ability by the Spirit of God to make a contribution. 'To each is given the manifestation of the Spirit for the common good' (1 Cor. 12:7).

It therefore becomes very important for each new believer to begin to seek out ways and means of making a contribution in the world and in the Church for Jesus Christ.

D.L. Moody, the great American evangelist, was accosted following a sermon he had preached, by a woman who said, 'Dr Moody, you made no fewer than twenty-five grammatical errors in your sermon.' Moody replied: 'You're probably right, madam. I had no college education and my grammar is not too good. But such grammar as I know I have offered to Christ for His service.'

Can we offer our gifts and abilities, such as they may be, to the living God? Why not? You'll be amazed what He'll make of them!

AIM TO LOVE

The Corinthian Church had many gifts and skills in it, but Paul was worried about their defectiveness in love. It is an important challenge to each of us.

On the other hand, the hard fact is that it is very difficult to manifest true Christian love in a consistent way without consciously and constantly appropriating the power of the Holy Spirit. It is He who must bring forth this fruit in us and we must co-operate with Him in that process.

So Paul sums up what he is asking the Corinthians to do with these words, 'make love your aim' (1 Cor. 14:1).

A seminary professor of mine, during a time in his life when he had been a pastor, felt constrained to go to a family who had been bereaved.

He knocked at the door. A stricken, tear-filled woman opened it. 'O, pastor,' she said, 'I knew you'd come.'

She had felt able to count on the pastor's compassionate heart and on that love which for ever must remain the basic hallmark of the Christian.

Love will also call us into a deep caring for the needs and brokenness of the society around us. Hunger, oppression and injustice are the proper concerns of the mature Christian.

BE A GIVER

Another central expression of Christian love is generous financial giving. This is fundamental to the Christian life. In fact, giving is a basic mark of the Christian. Money and our use of it is a great barometer of where we are with God. In fact, I do not think we are truly converted to Christ until our pocket-book is converted to Him as well!

Not long after I was brought to Christian commitment as a university student I was taught by Christians in Cambridge to give a tenth of my money to Christ. I had never heard of this before, although I had been raised in the Church. But this was the norm in the Old Testament. I was told that while this may not be required so strictly as a legal thing in the New Testament, nevertheless it provides a beautiful standard and point of departure for us and many blessings flow from it (see Malachi 3:10).

Being as broke and impoverished as most of my student friends, and often more so, as I was operating on vastly less than what was considered feasible for an overseas student, I had many opportunities through those years to put this principle to the test.

Once while studying French in Paris during a vacation, I ran out of money when I put my last two shillings, as my normal weekly tithe, into the collection.

Imagine my inner emotions when, just a few hours later, a friend, who knew nothing of my plight, gave me an enormous box of groceries. Having staggered back to my dingy little garret on the Avenue Victor Hugo near the Arc de Triomphe, I calculated the financial cost of the groceries I had just received. They added up to a sum approximately 200 times greater than the little coins with which I had rather reluctantly parted company a few hours previously!

A few days later a ten-pound cheque arrived in the mail from my dear mother back in South Africa. It had been sent two weeks previously. 'I woke last night,' she said, 'and felt a deep compulsion to send you some money. Hope it comes in handy!'

Bless her! It was enough to see me through with food, simple fare admittedly, for the rest of my stay in Paris! What a great lesson and principle I discovered.

I would therefore encourage you right away to decide that as a believer now you will begin cheerfully to tithe your income to Christian work. This may be directly to your church or to a Christian organisation or a bit to each.

WHEN WE TUMBLE

Let me alert you in conclusion to the fact that tumbles and slips will come. It won't all be plain sailing. Certainly you won't ever have a week such as the one conveyed in that absurd children's song:

On Monday I am happy,
On Tuesday full of joy,
On Wednesday I have peace within which nothing can destroy,
On Thursday and on Friday, I am walking in the light,
Saturday is heaven below,
And Sunday's always right!

Well, I've never had a week like that, and if you have, please write and tell me how you did it!

No, there will be ups and downs and lapses into old sins or habits. What then?

The answer is – bounce back. Like a boxer who gets knocked down, don't let yourself be knocked out! The way we prevent this is by coming back quickly and regularly to God in confession.

Writes St John: 'If we *confess* our sins He [God] is faithful and just to forgive us our sins and cleanse us from all unrighteousness' (1 John 1:9). As we come back to God in prayer and say we are sorry and determined to do better, God for His part does two things. Firstly He forgives. Secondly, He cleanses.

If as John says, we 'walk in the light' with God and with each other, then 'the blood of Jesus His Son cleanses us from all sin' (1 John 1:7).

Roy Hession, the British writer, has said:

> Not only where there is *need*, there is God, but where there is sin, there is Jesus – and that is something more wonderful. There is not always something blameworthy in a need, and we can understand God being touched and drawn by humanity's need. But humanity's sin, surely that does not draw Him, except in judgment. But no – just because God is what He is, and Jesus is what He is, and grace is what it is, it is gloriously true, where there is sin, there is always Jesus – seeking to forgive sin and recover all the damage that it has caused. He is not shocked by human failure: rather He is at home in it, drawn by it, knowing what to do about it, for He in Himself and in His blood is the answer to it all.[54]

So if when you tumble, get back quickly to Jesus in confession and repentance. He'll take care of the rest.

CONCLUSION

The Christian life is the adventure of all adventures because it not only makes life in the here and now thrilling and exciting and demanding but it promises us at the end of the day an entry into that presence of the living God which is beyond all our imaginings. Paul says that 'Eye has not seen, nor ear heard, neither has there entered into the heart of man, the things which God has prepared for them that love him' (1 Cor. 2:9 AV).

Whatever heaven is all about, it is certainly going to be majestic. One young teenager came to me with a song she had written entitled 'Heaven's going to be a Blast!' The song, I fear, won't exactly become a twentieth-century classic, but it certainly expresses a great truth! A glorious life beyond this life is something which we cannot conceive of at the present time. But it is real. I believe that with all my heart. The Apostle was feeling towards this reality when he said, 'I consider that the sufferings of this present time are not worth comparing with the glory that is to be revealed to us' (Rom. 8:18). Likewise, the Apostle John in his vision of the life beyond could write in majestic terms 'of a new heaven and a new earth' where God will dwell with His people and they with Him:

And he will wipe away every tear from their eyes, and death shall be no more, neither shall there be mourning nor crying nor pain any more, for the former things have passed away. And he who sat upon the throne said, 'Behold, I make all things new'. Also he said, 'Write this, for these words are trustworthy and true.' And he said to me, 'It is done! I am the Alpha and the Omega, the beginning and the end' (Rev. 21:4-6).

Yes, Jesus is indeed the Alpha and the Omega, the beginning and the end. What a glorious thing to follow Him as our all in all!

I have personally found knowing Jesus to be the most significant and meaningful thing in all of life. My sincere prayer is that you who have walked with me through these pages may have come to this conclusion too.

May each of us follow Him, in the words of David Livingstone, with 'No Reservations – No Regret – and No Retreat'.

Appendix: The New Testament and other manuscripts – a comparison

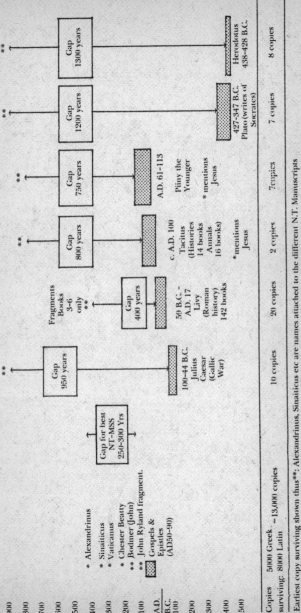

1000							
900							
800					Gap 1200 years **		Gap 1300 years **
700							
600			Gap 750 years **				
500	* Alexandrinus						
400	* Sinaiticus			Gap 800 years **	427-347 B.C. Plato (writes of Socrates)		Herodotus 438-428 B.C.
300	* Vaticanus						
200	* Chester Beatty	Gap 400 years **					
100	** Bodmer (John)			A.D. 61-113 Pliny the Younger * mentions Jesus			
A.D.	** John Ryland fragment. Gospels & Epistles (AD50-90)	Gap 950 years **		c. A.D. 100 Tacitus (Histories 14 books Annals 16 books) * mentions Jesus			
B.C. 100	Gap for best NT-MSS 250-300 Yrs	100-44 B.C. Julius Caesar (Gallic War)	Fragments Books 3-6 only ** 59 B.C. – A.D. 17 Livy (Roman history) 142 books				
200							
300							
400							
500							

Copies surviving:	5000 Greek. = 13,000 copies 8000 Latin	10 copies	20 copies	2 copies	? copies	7 copies	8 copies

Earliest copy surviving shown thus **; Alexandrinus, Sinaiticus etc are names attached to the different N.T. Manuscripts.

(by Norman Allchin, Acorn Press, Canberra 1981, p.8).

Notes

1. *Playboy* magazine, February 1963.
2. *Time* magazine, January 24, 1964.
3. *Time* magazine, April 16, 1965.
4. Eccles. 2:12–17 LB.
5. *To Be or Not To Be*, Duncan Williams, Davis-Poynter, London, 1974, p. 75.
6. Eccles. 2:17 LB.
7. Eccles. 2:18 RSV.
8. Eccles. 2:20 RSV.
9. 2 Cor. 5:17 AV.
10. Luke 16:31 AV.
11. John 7:17 LB.
12. Ps. 14:1 NAS.
13. *Reasons for Faith*, Oliver Barclay, Inter-Varsity Press, London, 1974, p. 23.
14. *Fearfully and Wonderfully Made*, Dr Paul Brand and Phillip Tancey, Hodder & Stoughton, London, 1981, p.25.
15. Ps. 139:14 AV.
16. Eccles. 11:5 RSV.
17. *The Medusa and the Snail*, Lewis Thomas, Allen Lane, London, 1980, p.00.
18. ibid. p. 00.
19. *Nature, Man and God*, William Temple, Macmillan & Co., London, 1964, p.129.
20. *The Mysterious Universe*, Sir James Jeans, p.149.
21. Temple, op. cit., p.132.
22. Jeans, op. cit., p.148.
23. *Priestland, Right and Wrong*, Programme One by Gerald Priestland. A series for Channel 4, South &

South East Communications Ltd. (TV5), Southampton, 1982.

24. *The Christian View of Science and Scripture*, Bernard Ramm, Paternoster Press, Exeter, 1955, pp.150–1.

25. *Understanding the Bible*, J.R.W. Stott, Scripture Union, London, 1972, p.63.

26. See *A General Introduction to the Bible*, Norman L. Geister and William E. Nix, Moody Press, Chicago, 1968, p.365.

27. *The New Testament Documents: Are They Reliable?* Prof. F.F. Bruce, Inter-Varsity Press, Downer Grove, Illinois, 1964, p.16ff.

28. *The New Testament in the Original Greek*, F.J.H. Hort and B.F. Westcott, Macmillan Co., New York, 1881, Vol. 1, p.561.

29. Quoted in *Recent Discoveries in Bible Lands*, William Albright, Funk & Wagnalls, New York, 1955, p.136.

30. *The Bearing of Recent Discovery on the Trustworthiness of the New Testament*, Sir William Ramsay, Hodder & Stoughton, London, 1915, p.222.

31. *The Acts of the Apostles*, E.M. Blaiklock, Eerdmans Pub. Co., Grand Rapids, 1959, p. 89.

32. *Rivers in the Desert: History of Negev*, Nelson Glueck, Jewish Publications Society of America, Philadelphia, 1969, p.31.

33. *What Mean These Stones?* Millar Burrows, Meridian Books, New York, 1956, p.1.

34. Quoted in *Can I Trust My Bible?* Howard Vos, Moody Press, Chicago, 1963, p.176.

35. 1 John 1:1–4 LB.

36. Col. 1:15–17 LB.

37. Quoted in *You Must Be Joking*, Michael Green, Hodder & Stoughton, London, 1976, p.72.

38. *Who Moved the Stone?* Frank Morison, Faber & Faber Ltd., London, 1958, p.26.

39. *The Gospel According to St. Mark*, H.B. Swete,

Macmillan & Co. Ltd., London, 1898, p.339.

40. *101 Proofs of the Deity of Christ from the Gospels*, F.J. Meldan, The Christian Victory Pub. Co., Grand Rapids, 1969, p.49.

41. Quoted in *Basic Christianity*, Revd. John Stott, Inter-Varsity Press, Downer Grove, Illinois, 1971, p.47.

42. Quoted in *Man Alive*, Michael Green, Inter-Varsity Press, Downer Grove, Illinois, 1968, pp. 53–4.

43. *The Helper*, Catherine Marshall, Hodder & Stoughton Ltd., London, 1978, p.81.

44. *The Dust of Death*, Os Guinness, Inter-Varsity Press, London, 1973, p.299.

45. *The Miracles*, by H. Richard Casdorph, *Logos*, Plainfield, New Jersey, 1976, p.16.

46. ibid., p.93.

47. ibid., pp.97–8.

48. ibid., p.95.

49. The physician handling the case of Ray Jackson made his report as follows (see pp.93–96 in *The Miracles*, H. Richard Casdorph):

This 45-year-old bank executive had a left nephrectomy in December, 1972, following hematuria and histologic diagnosis was adenocarcinoma. Following painful swelling of the left fourth finger, X-rays in March, 1974, demonstrated metastatic disease and on March 4th the digit was amputated confirming the radiologic impression. By late April he had severe pains in the right anterior rib-cage and in the left ischium. A bone scan showed abnormalities in the sternum at T-12-L-1, in the left pelvis, in the right S-I joint and in the fibula. Provera therapy was initiated 30mg a day.

Within one week of initiating Provera therapy and following a religious experience in Florida when he went to see Kathryn Kuhlman, all pain subsided and irradiation therapy which had been planned for the left ischium was not given. Since then he has felt quite well without pain, cough, shortness of breath, weight loss, or intercurrent illness.

Skeletal survey showed remarkable 'healing' of the lesion in the left ischium and similar increase in density in a former lytic site in the medical portion of the left ileum. During that same October visit, Ray Jackson was subjected to a metastatic survey, X-rays of the bones including all long bones.

The X-ray department reported the following:

The current examination including a lateral view of the skull, AP and lateral views of the spine, AP view of the pelvis and views of the proximal humeri and femora were compared with representative prior radiograms. *Healing* is noted of the previously described metastatic focus in the left ischium. No other metastatic foci can be identified. Despite the history afforded of a positive bone scan in the T-12-L-1 area in the left pelvis and right sacroiliac joints, no definite metastatic foci can be seen in these regions.

The diagnosis on this lab report was as follows:

1.   Healing of the previously described metastatic focus of the left ischium.
2.   No other metastatic foci are identified.

A return note by a member of the urologic department dated 10/17/74 stated the following:

The patient states after I last saw him he apparently had bone scans that showed five different lesions involving the ribs and part of the pelvis. They were apparently metastatic. He was initially going to receive cobalt therapy but over a weekend he went to some religious revival and his pain disappeared. He came back on the following day and on May 1st, he was put on Provera 10mg. t.i.d. and has been fine since. He had lost over 20 pounds prior to starting the Provera but he has gained all that back and a little more. He is now playing golf, exercises well, feels perfect in general. On examination he looks to be in excellent health.

50.   *Fear No Evil,* David Watson, Hodder & Stoughton, London, 1984, p.153.
51.   ibid., p.159.
52.   *A Genuinely Human Existence,* Stephen Neill, Constable & Co. Ltd., London, 1959, Chapter IV.
53.   *A Severe Mercy,* Sheldon Vanauken, Hodder & Stoughton, London, 1979, p.91.
54.   *We Would See Jesus,* Roy Hession, Christian Literature Crusade, Eastbourne, 1958, p.29.

Michael Cassidy

BURSTING THE WINESKINS

Michael Cassidy's personal quest for a deeper understanding and experience of the Holy Spirit. Fast moving
events are woven together with biblical experience as
Michael Cassidy combines theology and experience in this
witness to the power of the Spirit's ministry. Addressed
equally to both those involved in Renewal and those
outside the movement, he seeks to encourage Chritians
from many different backgrounds, and explores the close
connection between the Holy Spirit, evangelism and
social action.

Michael Green

NEW LIFE, NEW LIFESTYLE

A new life means a new lifestyle. Michael Green points the way forward for the new believer with clarity and infectious enthusiasm.

'Having found Christ, we want to explore him more and more, and give ourselves over to him in every department of our lives. That is the very heart of the Christian life: getting to know him better, and working out the implications of it in our behaviour and attitudes, our career and relationships.'